Watch the Rope

Watch the Rope

by W.E. Morriss

Cover design by Terry Gallagher/Doowah Design
Author photo by John Morriss

The aerial photograph (pages v and vi) © May 10, 1948. Her Majesty the
Queen in Right of Canada, reproduced from the collection of the National
Air Photo Library with permission of Natural Resources Canada.
All other photos and illustrations courtesy of the Department of Archives &
Special Collections, University of Manitoba

Published with the generous assistance of the Manitoba Arts Council
and The Canada Council.

Printed and bound in Canada by Les Ateliers Graphiques Marc Veilleux

Canadian Cataloguing in Publication Data

Morriss, E.
    Watch the rope

ISBN 0-920486-25-8

    1. Executions and executioners–Manitoba.
2. Trials–Manitoba. 3. Capital punishment. I. Title

HV8699.C2M67 1996 364.6'6'097127 C96-900662-4

In memory of Sheriff D.C.M. (Murray) Kyle
who cautioned me to watch the rope.

Table of Contents

Foreword

A fresh southerly wind brought unusually mild temperatures to Manitoba on January 5, 1946. The thermometer rose to just below freezing, offering a pleasant respite from Winnipeg's normal deep freeze at the outset of the new year.

At No. 5 Release Centre on the east side of Winnipeg's airport, then known as Stevenson's Field, I was undergoing the final phase of my discharge as a Flying Officer in the Royal Canadian Air Force. It seemed a long time since the day in early June 1940, when my steps were diverted across Portage Avenue to the RCAF recruiting office in the Lindsay Building on Notre Dame Avenue. France had fallen the previous day, and the decision to enlist had been made on the spur of the moment.

Now, after over five years, there were new decisions to be made in a changed and uncertain world. Nothing was the same, nor could it ever be again. I had returned to a city and a home that, in outward respects, were little changed. But, the companions of my youth were scattered. Some, including a brother, had not been as lucky as myself and had not returned. There were no threads to pick up, and the tight camaraderie that had bound squadrons, and more particularly aircrews together, was in the past. There was relief that the war was over and the killing had stopped, but confusion and uncertainty clouded the future.

On that January day, I had no inkling that I would shortly stumble into a newspaper career as a reporter, nor that a grim event late that same night would play a part in that new career. Shortly after 11 p.m. two bullets snuffed out the life of a 13-year-old boy. At 8:15 a.m. the next morning a yardman switched on the light in one of the coal bins at Moore's coal and wood yard at 150 Clarke Street in Winnipeg's Fort Rouge district. Huddled in the bin was the body of Roy Ewan McGregor. The victim of a homosexual attack, he had been shot in the stomach and the forehead. That discovery was to touch off one of the most intensive manhunts in the history of Winnipeg crime. It would end almost three years later when 24-year-old Michael Angelo Vescio dropped through the trap door in the execution chamber at Headingley jail on the outskirts of Winnipeg. But, not before he had repeated his crime and another 13-year-old boy had died.

As a reporter for the *Winnipeg Free Press*, I was to follow the trial of Vescio and those of six other condemned men through to the same grisly end. They were the last executions to be carried out in Manitoba.

I had thought that overseas service in the RCAF had hardened me to death. Nothing had prepared me, however, to witness those cold-blooded ritual killings, prescribed precisely according to time and place and committed in the name of society. It was a traumatic, numbing experience that remains vivid in the mind nearly five decades later. Each one became more emotionally draining than the last.

The expression, like that of a cornered animal, on the face of the first man I saw hanged still haunts me. The moment he was escorted into the execution chamber his eyes caught mine. There appeared to be a startled recognition of the reporter who had sat at the press table throughout his trials. Within the time that it takes to recite the Lord's Prayer, he was dead.

The tension within that place of horror was so intense that I felt physically ill. To make matters worse, I had strong doubts about his guilt at the time of his sentencing. Those doubts have been reinforced during the research undertaken to write this book.

That research was begun with the aim of outlining the circumstances that led each of the last seven men to die on the

gallows in Manitoba to their fate. The motivations behind the
crimes ranged from perversion, as in the case of Vescio, through
robbery, greed, passion, revenge and madness. Much has been
made of the death penalty as a deterrent to such violence. It can
only be pointed out that the death penalty was in effect, and was
being enforced with numbing regularity when the crimes outlined in this book were carried out. It did not deter the perpetra-
tors.

While the law governing homicide has changed drastically
since these events happened, there are many elements of the law
which still prevail today, and could come into play should the
death penalty ever be reintroduced in Canada.

It is hoped the reviewing of these case histories will be useful
to those participating in the recurring debate in Canada over the
restoration of capital punishment. Some may affirm that some, or
all, of the accused deserved their fate. I cannot agree that justice
was always done, nor that similar injustices cannot occur in the
future. A review of the notorious Donald Marshall case would
have been a useless exercise had the noose not been abolished in
Canada before his unjust conviction for a crime that he did not
commit.

I know that I could not have pulled the lever that plunged
those men to their deaths. I know too that I would never ask
someone else to do so in the name of the state. Nor do I believe
that anyone else in our society who is unwilling to undertake that
grisly task, should ask that another do it in their name.

It would now be fitting to express my appreciation to those who
assisted in the research and compilation of this book. My thanks
go to the Manitoba Arts Council, without whose assistance this
work might not have been undertaken. A word of appreciation is
also due to the staffs of the Manitoba Archives, the Manitoba
Legislative Library and the Winnipeg Public Library who aided
with source material on many occasions and to the office of the

Hon. Lloyd Axworthy for assistance with research carried out in Ottawa.

Finally, a special thanks to my wife Geraldine who aided in the research and as a fastidious editor would brook no errors or omissions.

Introduction

A deep reverence for human life is worth more than a thousand executions in the prevention of murder; and is, in fact, the greatest security of human life. The law of capital punishment whilst pretending to support this reverence, does in fact, tend to destroy it.

—John Bright

Twelve miles from the center of Winnipeg stands Headingley Jail surrounded by a pastoral setting of open farmland. Still intact within its red brick walls is one of the few permanent execution chambers ever built in Canada. Most gallows in other regions of the country were erected as the occasion demanded. They were crude, brutal devices which imposed an added cruel strain on both the condemned and the executioner. However, when Headingley Jail was finished in 1930, there was provision for an enclosed scaffold and pit, flanked by two cells isolated from the rest of the prison. As a complex for carrying out the task of breaking necks in the name of society, it was possibly the most efficient and humane—if such an act can ever be termed humane—available in Canada.

To reach that domain of death, you proceed from the warden's office beside the main entrance through two steel-barred doors, thence along a corridor beside a row of cells which open onto a common area separated from the corridor by more steel bars. At the end is a solid steel door set into a blank wall.

The guard inserts a large, wide key into a slot in the door and it creaks open. Within is a chamber some 24 feet square and nine feet high. Its brick walls are painted a light green, which in daylight reflect the light from a row of windows on the south wall of the wing containing the execution chamber. Around the room is a walkway some three feet wide, separated by a wooden rail from a raised plank platform. It was here that witnesses to the execution stood. On the east wall is another steel door which opens directly into a cell where condemned prisoners spent their last days.

Dominating the room is the gallows. Having a beam laminated from three two-by-six-inch planks, it is supported at either end by six-by-six-inch posts. Immediately below that beam there was once a pair of heavy-hinged doors. Today that space is covered by a temporary plywood floor, and the steel lever that withdrew the bolts to let those doors swing down with a thunderous bang is gone. Parallel to the west wall a wooden staircase leads down to a pit below. It is a concrete-floored room of the same dimensions as the chamber above. Save for some exposed plumbing on the east wall, and a steel door in the southeast corner leading to the outside, the room is completely bare. The heavy trap doors, each suspended by three massive hinges, now hang down in the open position beneath the exposed bridging of the upper execution chamber floor. In years past, the witnesses and the coroner's jury gathered here waiting as the prison doctor moved forward from time to time to place a stethoscope on the chest of a body, with arms pinioned behind the back and legs bound with a strap, suspended by a rope extending up through the trap door to the dark green beam above. If all had gone well the head, covered by a black hood, was twisted at an incongruous angle to the right, and while the heart would beat on for some minutes before the doctor could declare life extinct, the neck had been snapped and clinical death had been instantaneous.

All did not always go well however. There were occasions when the witnesses would be restrained from going down to the lower pit while the victim jerked spasmodically on the end of the rope. On other occasions the floor and walls could be splattered with blood, for Canada had an abysmal record of botched hangings; a record probably unsurpassed by any other civilized nation. Canada's official executioners were too often incompetent bunglers.

Buried inconspicuously in the top right hand corner of Page 7 of the *Manitoba Free Press* of August 26, 1926, was one record of that incompetence:

> Bungled in a horrible manner, the hanging of Dan Prociw, murderer of Annie Cardno, his common-law wife, at 57 1/2 Heaton Avenue March 16, was carried out at dawn yesterday in the yard of the provincial jail. Too long a drop was given by the hangman, and the head of the doomed man was severed from the body. Prociw met his death calmly.

Prociw may well have been calm, as that short account so succinctly ended, but the executioner was not. Arthur Bartholomew English, alias Arthur Ellis, had run from the gallows crying; "I knew it. I knew it." Scarcely had he pulled the lever to spring the trap than the rope came snapping back through the opening. On that day Ellis, who had acted as chief executioner, or as an assistant, at some 600 hangings in a career extending from England to the Middle East and thence to Canada, had been faced with a man of 240 pounds grown soft in jail and with a neck that was not muscular in proportion. Another hangman known as "Camille" faced the same problem on June 17, 1952, when he dropped stockily built 220-pound Henry Malanik into the pit at Headingley Jail. That hanging, the last carried out in Manitoba, was also a bloody affair.

While gory, it can be argued that death was mercifully sudden in too long a drop. When the executioner misjudged the length of the rope on the short side, it could be a lingering death. All too often, the convicted man or woman was suspended struggling and gasping for breath at the end of a slowly moving rope.

English also officiated at possibly the most shocking incident involving a short drop. At 7:55 a.m. on September 12, 1919, 23-year-old Antonio Sprecage dropped through the trap on the temporary scaffold erected in the yard of Montreal's Bordeaux Jail. Eight minutes later the jail doctor declared that the heart had stopped beating. He instructed that Sprecage be cut down. But, the neck had not been broken. Convulsive tremors began to wrack the body. It was not until 9:02 a.m. that the prison doctor could officially pronounce Sprecage dead—one-hour-and-seven-minutes after he had dropped.

Equally horrifying was the work of an amateur hangman, W.A. Doyle, at the county jail in Woodstock Ontario, on October 26, 1922. Bennie Swim, convicted of a double murder, dropped through the trap at 5 a.m. Shortly afterwards, Doyle went into the pit and declared Swim to be "deader than a doornail." The body was lowered, carried down a corridor and placed on a cot. Thomas Griffin, the prison doctor, then found that the neck had not been broken; that Swim was still breathing and rapidly improving. Faced with a terrible decision, Sheriff Albion Foster had Swim taken to the scaffold and hanged again. This time Doyle was successful in the task for which he had volunteered. It was estimated however that between 50 and 60 minutes passed between the first and second hangings. So much for the myth that a condemned person cannot be hanged twice.

The long career of English as Canada's official hangman began on December 12, 1913, in Kamloops, British Columbia. His final performance took place at Montreal's Bordeaux Jail in 1937, when he was 71 years of age. A triple execution, it was an unmitigated disaster. The condemned trio included Mrs. Tomasino Sarao and two male accomplices, Leone Gagliardi and Angelo Donafrie, convicted in the death of Mrs. Sarao's husband.

First to climb the long flight of stairs from the jail courtyard to the platform, erected at the second floor window level of the jail, were Gagliardi and Donafrie. With the guards holding a fainting Gagliardi erect, the two men plunged through the trap back-to-back. Neither neck was broken. Both died of strangulation. A short while later Mrs. Sarao ascended the stairs showing far more composure than Gagliardi had done. English was given her weight as 145 pounds. It had been that when she entered the jail, but she had put on 42 pounds since that time. A second after the bolts were drawn the rope came flying back through the trap, slapped against the overhead beam, then dropped back through the hole. Mrs. Sarao had been decapitated.

After that triple bungle, a boycott of English took place. No sheriff was willing to call upon him again. A Montreal police captain found English, alone and friendless, dying in his rented room in early 1938. Taken to Ste Jeanne D'Arc Hospice, he died penniless shortly after.

English's long career as the principal Canadian hangman led to the popular myth that all hangmen had their identity cloaked in the name of "Mr. Ellis." It was not always so. His predecessor John Robert Radclive, who learned his trade as an apprentice to the famous hangman William Marwood in England, carried out his grim trade under his own name between 1890 and 1912 in Canada. Radclive scorned the use of a black hangman's hood, normally used when a hanging had to take place in the open in the prison yard. He always appeared elegantly dressed in a black Prince Albert coat, which became his trademark. He said in an interview in 1912 that he had hanged 132 persons:

> My family deserted me and changed their names, but I kept right on with the job, because I argued with myself that, if what I was doing was wrong, then the government of my country was wrong. I held that I was the Minister of Justice at a hanging and that if I was a murderer, then he also was a murderer.

Strangely both Radclive and English, though initiated to their grisly trade in England, never favoured the Marwood noose, although its use in England had consistently proven that it resulted in instantaneous death by dislocation of the neck. When he became official hangman in Great Britain, William Marwood abandoned the former stiff rope of about one-and-a-half-inches in diameter for a more flexible rope of about half that diameter. The former heavy knot, formed by tying several slip knots in succession, was replaced by a metal ring around which the end of the rope was turned and secured by binding. A leather washer behind the ring kept the noose in place and did not allow it to slip.

By experimentation, Marwood found that cleaner dislocations were obtained by placing the metal ring under the point of the chin. He was also the first hangman to work out a series of tables according to the weight of the victim. The principle was to judge the length of the rope, which was earlier stretched by repeated drops using a bag of cement, so that the neck was broken without the risk of decapitation.

Unfortunately, neither Radclive nor English favoured the Marwood noose, preferring to stick with the traditional hangman's knot placed behind the left ear. Consequently, some estimates have placed the percentage of strangulations to dislocations in Canada as being about equal. While, officially, in the English speaking Western World, it was the duty of the sheriff of the judicial district in which the prisoner was held to carry out the executions, the common procedure was to arrange for a professional hangman to perform the mechanical function. A notable exception to that custom was Grover Cleveland, the only president of the United States to be re-elected after being defeated. Cleveland, who served as president from 1885 to 1889 and again from 1893 to 1897, had earlier been elected as the sheriff of Erie County in New York State in 1870. When the county had to execute two convicted murderers, Cleveland insisted on springing the trap personally, declaring that, under the law, it was the duty of the sheriff, and he would not ask anyone to do what he was unwilling to do himself. In light of the inept performance of some professional hangmen, the former U.S. president's moral rectitude may have overcome his good judgement.

Because of that aforementioned tendency of hangmen to bungle executions in Canada, it is little wonder that Arthur English wrote in 1937 that "seven out of ten sheriffs attending an execution shut their eyes until the trap was sprung." Fortunately, Sheriff D.C.M. "Murray" Kyle, of the Eastern Judicial District of Manitoba, was not one of them. It was from him that I learned that hangings did not always go according to plan. The first hanging I was assigned to cover was that of Lawrence Deacon on April 16, 1948. Almost overcome with the tension, I closed my eyes. Then, hearing the crash of the gallows doors, I looked down at my watch to catch the precise time for my report. When Murray asked how I felt afterwards, I told him I could not watch. He had some advice:

> Don't close your eyes. Watch the rope. If it begins to jiggle around, don't go downstairs, at least not for some time. If it snaps back, for God's sake don't go downstairs. You can get the details from someone else.

It was valuable advice. Over the next several years I was to see the rope jerk convulsively on one occasion. Fortunately, I never saw it snap back. I was equally lucky because another unfortunate reporter volunteered to take my place at the hanging of Henry Malanik. Sadly I neglected to pass along Murray's advice with the official pass. I don't think he ever volunteered for anything again. His written report had few details of what happened. He was apparently too distraught by the bloody events to take notes.

It was an area in which we were derelict in any event during my tenure on the Law Courts beat. The public was never given any gory details. It seemed that a society which could try a man, or woman, and condemn them to "be hung by the neck until you are dead," had to be spared any unpleasantness associated with that decision. A conspiracy of silence appeared to exist if anything untoward happened. Both the *Winnipeg Free Press* and the *Winnipeg Tribune* dutifully reported that the hanging had taken place, how the condemned person had faced the ordeal, and a host of other details. But, if the hanging was bungled, there was no sign. That is unless you were knowledgeable enough to read between the lines by noting the time the trap was sprung and the time that passed before the prison doctor pronounced the victim dead.

In retrospect that concession to public sensitivity was a mistake. Had the details been reported fully, and the horror impressed on the public mind, it might have accelerated the move to abolition in Canada.

As early as 1886, public concern over reported incidents of recurring mishaps led to the appointment of a committee of enquiry in Great Britain. Following the report of that committee, precautions were instituted in Britain well before the turn of the century. As a result, Sir Ernest Gowers, chairman of a Royal Commission on Capital Punishment in Britain from 1949 to 1953, could report that:

Since these precautions were taken, there is no record in the Home Office of any failure or mishap in connection with an execution, and in the opinion of that department execution by hanging, as now carried out, can be regarded as speedy and certain.

Evidence that Sir Ernest's assertion was correct appears to be borne out by the prominent abolitionist Arthur Koestler, whose book *Reflections on Hanging* created a storm of controversy and heated debate in the British House of Commons, and was credited with playing a major role in the abolition of the death penalty in Britain in 1969. Koestler's intensive research turned up only one incident on which to base a claim of evidence that a hanging was bungled. However, it was an inference only, and far from positive. Koestler noted that a coroner's report on a hanging contained the words, "noose slipped on jaw."

As a comparison to the abominable record in Canada, the British experience deserves study. There appear to be two main reasons executions in Britain were more successfully and humanely carried out. British hangmen were carefully trained, and the law considered the physical condition of the condemned person.

British legislators in 1886 recognized that, among murderers condemned to death, there were occasionally some whose condition made it undesirable that the execution should be carried out, "because some scandalous thing might happen—a person's head might come off because the jaw was shot away or some gruesome development might happen which would shock public opinion rather than show that the law had been vindicated."

Thus, if the prison doctor, or the hangman, reached the conclusion that some "untoward" incident might occur, the death sentence was commuted to life imprisonment. Sir Ernest, who was a retentionist when he accepted the chairmanship of the Royal Commission in 1949, but who had become an abolitionist by the end of the hearings, had a wry comment on that element of the British law:

A future student of the strange customs of the natives of Britain in the twentieth century will find few that will seem more quaint than that a decision between the death penalty and a less severe punishment should sometimes have depended not on the gravity of the offence, but on the shape of the offender's neck.

Care was also exercised in the selection and training of

hangmen in Britain. A panel of six names was kept by the prison commissioners, and applicants seeking to have their names placed on that list were carefully screened. Those chosen attended classes at Pentonville Prison, where they were reported on and a selection made. Classes lasted for one week and the trainees carried out a dummy execution. After graduation, the applicant had to serve for a fixed period as an assistant to an experienced hangman. The result of these precautions was a remarkable efficiency. In British prisons, as in the complex at Headingley Jail, the condemned cell adjoined the execution chamber with a door opening directly into it. Evidence given before the 1949 Royal Commission in Britain was that the time between the entry of the executioner into the condemned cell and the pulling of the lever to spring the trapdoors was normally about ten seconds. My own timing of six executions at Headingley Jail, including one double hanging, was that less than 30 seconds passed between the time the condemned man entered the chamber and the trap was sprung.

Evidence given at the Royal Commission hearings in Britain was almost unanimous that: "hanging is certain, painless, simple and expeditious." After examining and comparing other methods of execution, notably electrocution and gassing, the commission reached the conclusion that no better method could be devised that would be practical. It was with reluctance that they had to reject the alternative of lethal injection because of its practical difficulties. Sir Ernest commented: "Thus a method of execution whose special merit was thought to be that it was peculiarly degrading is now defended on the ground that it is uniquely humane."

That conclusion reached in Britain appears to be borne out by horror stories emanating from the United States in recent years. There has been a long search in the retentionist states for some means of administering painless death. Lethal injection, the administering of a witch's brew of drugs to the condemned person, has been touted by many as the most civilized way to take a life. Eyewitness accounts, however, suggest that such executions may have become less and not more humane.

In each of the alternatives to hanging there is a prolonged period of preparation to be undergone by the condemned person, adding to the terrible stress on the prisoner, as well as the executioner and the witnesses. Given the questionable success of those choices, and the prolongation of terror for the prisoner in his last moments, the question can validly be raised as to whether the exercise is to distance the executioner from his act, instead of a search for a more humane way of disposing of the condemned. The executioner who starts the flow of lethal drugs into the arm of the prisoner hides behind a one-way glass, or a wall with a hole in it. The man who throws the switch to crisp the man strapped in the electric chair is hidden, as is the man who turns the gas cock to suffocate society's victim.

Is the person who activates the final step in a ritual killing by the State seeking anonymity from the prisoner? Or is he seeking to hide his part in the ritual from the society that decreed that the sentence of death must be carried out? Those who strap a person into an electric chair, or shave the victim's head and legs to attach electrodes to the body, or insert an intravenous needle into the arm of a condemned person, are a part of society's retribution. If capital punishment is the will of the people, surely the executioners, they who finish the circle of the law, need not hide. Those who uphold capital punishment should honour and respect them. They seldom do. The wives of both Radclive and English left them after they found that their husbands were not travelling salesmen, as they claimed, to cover their true vocation. English also lost his job as a bartender in a prominent Toronto men's club when his identity as a hangman was discovered. The puritanical members, most of whom approved heartily of capital punishment, could not be tainted by being served by an executioner.

Those of our federal legislators, and others, who still seek a return of the death penalty, often try to salve the conscience of society by advocating a change in the method of execution to create an illusion of compassion. All the evidence shows however that with all its degrading implications, hanging within a proper facility and with suitable safeguards, is the quickest, most efficient, and therefore, most humane way of despatching a condemned human being to eternity.

Most advocates of capital punishment seek its return as a deterrent to others who may consider taking a human life. Deterrence as justification for the noose dates from the days when capital punishment was imposed for a wide range of offences. It must have been heartening to one man sentenced for stealing sheep in the early nineteenth century to be unctuously reminded by a judge in Upper Canada that he was not being hung for stealing sheep, "but so that other sheep shall not be stolen." The learned judge might have been startled to learn that, in the three years preceding the abolishment of capital punishment for cattle stealing in Britain in 1820, 113 persons were charged with that offence and three were executed, whereas in the three years following the abolition only 67 persons were charged with cattle stealing.

There is also the oft-told tale of the public hangings at Tyburn Prison in Britain when picking pockets was a capital offence. The light-fingered cutpurses of the day counted it the best time to ply their trade when the crowd's attention was diverted by the drop of the unfortunate felon. Even as a fellow pickpocket dangled from the gibbet before their eyes, they lifted purses with abandon.

Penologists and others have pointed out that, in order for any form of punishment to have a deterrent effect, it must be applied without exception and expeditiously. Cases which drag through the courts, with the inevitable hope of commutation, or even freedom through a pardon, can have no deterrent effect. One prominent penologist argued that the hope aroused in the minds of criminals by one pardon outweighs the fear aroused by 20 executions.

In 1987, Members of Parliament were again hearing all the old arguments in Ottawa, as a determined group of backbenchers, claiming to be backed by strong public sentiment, tried to restore the death penalty in Canada. The Tory backbenchers were attempting to reverse a trend that began early in this century when Robert Bickerdike, a Montreal financier and underwriter who represented the federal riding of St. Lawrence-Montreal from 1904 to 1917, made a determined effort to have the death penalty abolished. Declaring that capital punishment was "essentially murder, a blot on Christianity, a blight on religion and a reproach to any nation that allows it to remain on the statute book," he made his first attempt on February 5, 1914. His private member's bill was voted down after scant debate, and he had little more success with later bills in 1915, 1916 and 1917.

Given the tenor of the times, and the fact that Canada was in the midst of a bloody war, the failure of Bickerdike's initiatives was not surprising. However, Bickerdike kept a series of scrapbooks on bungled hangings in Canada, setting out in lurid detail the shortcomings and brutality of the way executions were carried out in Canada. That his revelations did not, as in Britain decades earlier, lead to an investigation and reform is testimony to the callous indifference of the majority of Canada's parliamentarians. That the bungling persisted without reform for another half century is indefensible.

Another try at reform came in April 1924 when Reverend William Irvine, MP for Calgary East, moved another private member's bill calling for abolition of the death penalty. It was debated briefly, but with Justice Minister Ernest Lapointe and Solicitor-General E.J. McMurray opposing it, the bill went down to defeat in a free vote that resulted in 29 voting for its adoption and 92 against it. (McMurray will appear in a far different role in the first chapter of this book.)

Following that there was a hiatus, and it was not until the late 1940s that an impetus for abolition of the death penalty really took root in Canada, primarily because of a proposal for a five-year moratorium in Great Britain. The first move in Ottawa came in 1948 when minor amendments were made to the Criminal Code in respect to infanticide. A new category of manslaughter was introduced in cases where an infant was killed by its mother while the balance of her mind was disturbed.

Ironically, the next real attempt to abolish capital punishment was started by W. Ross Thatcher, then MP for Moose Jaw and later premier of Saskatchewan, whose son is serving a life sentence for the murder of his former wife, following one of the most sensational trials in the history of Canadian courts. The elder Thatcher introduced a private member's bill in February 1950, aimed at ending the death penalty. After only a few hours of desultory debate, it was withdrawn when Thatcher saw its chances of acceptance were poor. He tried again in 1953 with a similar bill. This too was withdrawn, but only after Justice Minister Stuart Garson promised that the matter would be dealt with by a special committee working to revise the existing criminal law and produce a consolidated Criminal Code. Revision of the code did not deal with the question of capital punishment however, other than to suggest that it be a question for further study. Consequent to that recommendation a joint committee of the House and Senate was established. When that committee introduced its report in 1956, it recommended retention of the death penalty as the mandatory punishment for murder. However, there appeared to finally be a realization of the callous way the death penalty was being administered in Canada. The committee called for a centralized place of execution in each province and replacement of the gallows by the gas chamber. The latter proposal contrasts strangely with the findings of the Royal Commission in Britain. Possibly the Canadian legislators were influenced by the disastrous number of botched hangings in Canada, but did not enquire into the cause for the mishaps and the remedial action required.

There was also something surreal in one of the reasons quoted in the clause recommending replacement of hanging by a centrally located gas chamber. It noted the cost involved in erecting a scaffold in each prison on the rare occasion of an execution there. Were the considerations a matter of compassion or economy? Canadian hangmen, despite their ineptness in relation to their British counterparts, had at least shown concern for their victims by consistently calling for more humane facilities since before the turn of the century. Both Radclive and English had been dismayed by the lack of privacy at the open air scaffolds, and by the ordeal of the condemned prisoners who sometimes had to mount, or be carried up, as many as 17 steps to meet their fate.

In any event, the recommendations of the committee were not acted upon. Canada had entered the politically turbulent Diefenbaker-Pearson years. Having acted as defence counsel at many criminal trials in Saskatchewan, Prime Minister John Diefenbaker was a confirmed abolitionist. While there were some inconsistencies in the exercise of the prerogative of the Governor-in-Council to grant clemency, no doubt in an attempt to assuage the still pervasive retentionist faction in Parliament, Diefenbaker's Conservative cabinet began commuting death sentences as never before in the history of the courts in Canada.

Thus it was that governments of the late 1950s, and over the next generation, while proceeding timorously in the House of Commons, were moving aggressively through executive action toward abolition. The result was *de jure* retention of capital punishment on the statute book while *de facto* abolition ruled through commutation by order-in-council. Statistics compiled over an 80-year period, from 1881 to 1960 inclusive, showed that a person charged with murder in Canada had a 50-50 chance of being sentenced to death. Once sentenced there was another 50-50 chance of escaping execution. However, during the final five years of that period, from 1956 through 1960, a person charged with murder had only one chance in three of being sentenced to hang, and three chances in four of escaping the death penalty as 73 per cent of the sentences were commuted. Over that five years 191 persons were charged, 63 were sentenced to hang, of which 46 had their sentences commuted and 15 were hanged.

When the last two men died on the gallows in Canada at Toronto's Don Jail in the early hours of December 11, 1962, the death penalty was being used very sparingly. After the Liberals, under Lester Pearson, formed a new government in 1963, the moratorium by fiat became absolute. Although public opinion polls continued to show a strong preference for retention of the death penalty, and capital punishment stood on the statute books for a further 13 years to July 26, 1976, the federal cabinet steadfastly commuted every death sentence, no matter how heinous the offence.

Meanwhile, several bills had been debated in the Commons. The first real change in the law on homicide came in 1961, when the government, acting upon a committee report, divided murder into two categories—capital and non-capital. Capital offences, for which the death penalty was proscribed, included premeditated murder, the killing of a police officer or a prison guard, and murder committed in the commission of another offence. Other killings were non-capital with a maximum penalty of life imprisonment. The amendments made little difference since, under the former practice, juries always had the choice of reducing a murder charge to manslaughter. In any event, the cabinet was commuting all death sentences passed in the courts, and the mood for abolition was growing in Parliament. The result was a prolonged five-day debate in the Commons in 1966 before a motion calling for abolition was rejected by a vote of 143 to 112.

Then, on November 9, 1967, Solicitor-General L.T. Pennell introduced a bill narrowing the definition of capital murder to cases involving the killing of peace officers—policemen, prison guards and parole or probation officers. In a free vote, it passed by 114 to 67. There can be little doubt that the retentionists, dismayed at the five-year moratorium by cabinet intervention, hoped the narrowing of the rules might impose an imperative upon the prime minister and cabinet to, in effect, restore the death penalty at least along narrow lines. It was not to be. Prime Minister Pierre Trudeau and his cabinet continued to commute death sentences for the murder of police officers. Finally, on July 14, 1976, what had unofficially been in effect for almost 13 years became the law of the land. In another free vote, the House of Commons abolished the death penalty by a slim six-vote margin of 130 to 124.

That 13-year lag between the *de facto* abolition by fiat since 1962 and the *de jure* abolition in 1976, has produced some garbled and disjointed statistics in the continuing debate on whether the death penalty is a deterrent to homicide. Many participants in that debate choose to draw statistical comparisons using the legislated date of abolition, ignoring the obvious fact that an unenforced statute is no statute. This discrepancy has been further compounded by the fact that the death penalty had been used with progressive infrequency over the decade leading up to the last hangings in Canada in 1962. In the province of Manitoba for example, the last hanging was in 1952, some twenty-four years before the death penalty was officially lifted from the statute books.

Public debate continued, however, over more than a decade after the death penalty had been abolished; particularly after the 1982 trial and sentencing to life imprisonment of serial-killer Clifford Olson who murdered 11 young people in British Columbia. In the aftermath of that grisly series of killings of innocents, public agitation for return of the death penalty strengthened. Hence, during the 1984 general election campaign, Conservative Leader Brian Mulroney promised another free vote on the issue if his party formed the government. While personally opposed to a return of the death penalty, Prime Minister Mulroney partly fulfilled that promise in June 1987. A bill to begin a study into restoration was introduced. Debate on that bill culminated in the early hours of June 30, 1987, when the proposed study was rejected by 148 votes to 127.

Given the fact that the impetus for return of the death penalty has traditionally originated from the right, and that the Progressive Conservative Party held a record majority of 211 seats in the 282-member House of Commons, the vote, while not overwhelming, should normally have been expected to close the issue. It seems almost certain that such a propitious environment for the return of capital punishment is unlikely to present itself again. But the proponents of capital punishment appear not to have given up. There have been signs that they have been regrouping with the aim of again raising the issue in Parliament by calling for a national referendum.

It is hoped that what appears here may dissuade some ardent advocates of a return to the noose. As one who has been closely involved as a witness to court procedures at a period when the death penalty prevailed, I have little faith that the vaunted safeguards under our criminal law always prevail. Too often the fate of an accused rested on a whim or a chance of fate. The question of life or death, as I witnessed it, was often governed by which judge was assigned to preside at the trial. It could equally hinge on the philosophic outlook of a single juror, the prevailing and sometimes changing moods of public opinion, or a multitude of other factors.

The belief that an accused person will be accorded the benefit of that cornerstone of our judicial system, that the Crown must prove guilt beyond a reasonable doubt as a safeguard against wrongful conviction, cannot be substantiated in practice. Nor can it be readily assumed, despite advances in the art of psychiatry in this century that a mentally deranged person will not suffer the full prescribed weight of the law. The M'Naghten Rules, which for over 140 years have set forth the formula for assessing a defence of insanity, and still form a part of every judge's charge to the jury when such a defence is raised, are an anachronism. If the M'Naghten Rules are strictly applied as a test of mental incapacity, then it is almost impossible to sustain a defence of insanity.

During my tenure on the law courts beat I made the mistaken assumption that the M'Naghten Rules were one of the imbedded precedents in our common law. They are not. In a system of jurisprudence that lays almost obsessive emphasis on legal precedents, they are a unique anti-precedent. Arthur Koestler made the point that, since the M'Naghten Rules are an unprecedented curiosity in the history of the common law, they are technically not authority because they are not based on a trial. M'Naghten was not a judge. Rather he was a madman. A Protestant from Northern Ireland, M'Naghten was seized of the delusion that the Pope, the Jesuit Order and Britain's Prime Minister Sir Robert Peel were conspiring against him to bring about his death. Having purchased a pistol he stationed himself in Downing Street one day in 1843 to await the arrival of Peel whom he described as "the Prince of all-Evil." Since press photography did not then exist, he did not know what Peel looked like; so he mistakenly shot and killed Peel's secretary, Edward Drummond, when he chanced to walk by.

Although the term "psychiatry" had not yet been coined, eight medical witnesses were called at the trial. All concurred that M'Naghten was deprived of all restraint over his actions because of his delusion. Following that, Lord Chief Justice Tindal stopped the trial and instructed the jury to bring in a verdict of not guilty by reason of insanity, and M'Naghten was sent to an institution. That was a legal precedent. What followed was not. There followed a public outcry, particularly from the privileged classes who ventured that M'Naghten should have been hung, presumably to deter other lunatics from believing that Sir Robert Peel and the Pope were after their lives. The ponderous machinery of the House of Lords was brought into play, and their lordships prepared a questionnaire. Instead of being sent to the medical profession, it was distributed to the 15 High Court Judges of Britain. Fourteen of them responded with the opinion that M'Naghten should have been hanged, and their reasoning constituted the M'Naghten Rules.

The principles of that "anti-precedent" that have survived for almost a century-and-a-half as a rebuke from the Bench to the medical profession, are briefly that, to establish a defence on the grounds of insanity, it must be clearly proved that the accused was labouring under such a defect of reason, from disease of the mind, as not to know the nature and quality of the act he was doing, or, if he did know it that he did not know that he was doing wrong. Secondly, it was ruled that if a person labours under an insane delusion "he must be considered in the same situation as to responsibility as if the facts with respect to which the delusion exists were real."

That convoluted reasoning has been intoned time and again by learned trial judges, since the defence of insanity, or temporary loss of reasoning, is one of the most common types of defence put forward at murder trials. Sometimes the presiding judge, who must relate the M'Naghten rules in his charge to the jury, simplifies the jargon by stating that, if the accused was capable of forming an intent, then the defence of insanity cannot be upheld. Since, usually, the accused person has seized, or acquired in some way, a weapon to attack the deceased, it is *prima facie* evidence that an intent has been formed. Yet, as Koestler noted; "In the petrified forest of the law they [the M'Naghten Rules] stand rigid and indestructible."

Given the frequency that the M'Naghten Rules are enjoined in the defence of a person accused of murder, this brief review of their content and intent is important in relating the circumstances of some of the cases which follow. But, first let us deal with the concept that the guilt of an accused person "must be proven beyond reasonable doubt," in what might be called the case of the missing witness.

Below:
Lawrence Deacon maintained his innocence to the end, and thousands of Winnipeggers had extreme doubts as to his guilt. He is shown here leaving the court handcuffed to a sheriff's officer.

Above:
Mrs. Martha Perrault. She told Walter Stoney he didn't have the nerve to kill her. He did.

Left:
Detective Sergeant James E. Sims, who died from a shotgun blast fired by Walter Malanik, the last man to be hanged in Manitoba.

Below:
The entrance to Headingley Jail. Inside is one of the few permanent gallows complexes ever constructed in Canada.

Above:
Detectives are shown inspecting the spot where Walter Stoney threw himself in the path of a passing freight train a few yards north of Main Street in Winnipeg.

Left:
This was the Northern Taxi garage. The dark Chrysler immediately to the right of the door is the car in which cab driver Johann Johnson met his fate. Note the absence of a light on the roof.

Left:
1948 Aerial photo of Winnipeg.

Below:
This diagram, prepared for the *Winnipeg Free Press*, is of the Tuxedo area where Johann Johnson, Winnipeg taxicab driver, was found murdered. See Appendix (page 193) for more information.

Photograph number
A11320-205

Left:
The National Hotel, one of the seedy establishments facing onto North Main Street, where the body of Mrs. Martha Perrault was discovered.

Below:
R.C.M.P. officers are shown carefully recovering the hunting rifle used by Camille Allarie to gun down his employers William and Edith Delbridge in their farm home near Poplar Point.

Above:
Headingley Jail, on the banks of the Assiniboine River on the outskirts of Winnipeg, is shown in this aerial photo. The execution chamber is housed at the rear of the wing to the left.

Right:
The last man to be hanged in Manitoba, Henry Malanik, is shown being escorted from the court house by two of the Sheriff's officers. Malanik is the bareheaded man.

This is "Mr. X," Allan Cox, the "stool pigeon" whose evidence sent William Lusanko to the gallows while three of Lusanko's accomplices sat as free men in the court during the trial.

Chapter One

The Anniversary Party

This is no doubt the last opportunity I shall have of expressing publicly some of my thoughts. I have had made known to me all the steps that have been taken and all the efforts that have been made by so many persons in my behalf during the past two years, and I am deeply grateful and appreciate everything that has been done. I wish to thank my employers, Mr. and Mrs. H. J. Gray, who have had so much confidence in my innocence, and who have stood so loyally at my side, and who have helped my mother bear up under the strain.

I wish to thank the Deacon Defence Fund Committee, headed by Lt.-Col. G.M. Churchill, M.L.A., together with all the members of his committee, and all those who contributed to the fund.

I thank the Fort Garry Horse Association (10 C.A.R.), the M.L.A.'s who wired Ottawa on my behalf, the 15,000 people who signed the petition on my behalf, the numerous business firms and organizations that petitioned for clemency.

I understand that the newspapers of Winnipeg published the evidence presented at my trials and the argument on my appeals very fully and fairly, and helped in acquainting the public with my petition, and I therefore thank the *Winnipeg Free Press*, the *Winnipeg Tribune* and the *Winnipeg Citizen*.

I wish to thank especially my defence counsel, Hon. E. J. McMurray, K.C., and Harry Walsh for their constant efforts on my behalf, and for having expressed to me their sincere belief in my innocence.

My counsel have assured me that they will track down every clue that presents itself in an effort to clear my name.

I hope that this will be achieved during the lifetime of my mother.

I am requesting that this letter be publicized.

Within hours of signing that statement, Lawrence Sylvester Deacon, a 35-year-old veteran recently returned from overseas duty in the Second World War, died in the execution chamber at Headingley Jail. He dropped through the trap at 1:06 a.m. on April 16, 1948, two years after he had been charged with the iron bolt slaying of a Winnipeg taxi driver. At 1:19 a.m. Dr. E.K. Vann, the prison physician, nodded his head and the guards lowered the body from the scaffold.

The memory of that scene has haunted me for almost 50 years. As a young reporter it was the first time I witnessed an execution, and having covered the trials of Deacon and the subsequent appeals against his conviction, I had grave doubts that justice had been served. Today, after reviewing the newspapers of the period, court records, and reading and rereading the transcript of evidence, that nagging doubt as to his guilt has been reinforced.

Also, the discovery of aerial photographs taken about the time of the murder, which were listed as "confidential" at the time of the trial, shed new light on the spurious evidence that led to Lawrence Deacon's conviction for murder. Had those photographs been available to the defence, it is more than probable that Deacon would have been acquitted. I now firmly believe that an innocent man was hung.

Many members of the public, who followed the fate of Deacon through two trials over the two year period, apparently shared my misgivings and doubts about his guilt. Probably never before, or since, have Winnipeg citizens been so aroused over the imposition of the death penalty. The Public Archives of Canada attest to the intensity of the feelings provoked in the community. Still on file in Ottawa are 750 pages of petitions, bearing almost 15,000 signatures, calling for a reprieve or commutation of the death sentence. Included is one petition signed by seventy-five members of the legal profession, and one signed by a number of members of the Manitoba Legislature.

Today, the mystery remains as to why Justice Minister J.L. Ilsley and the cabinet of Prime Minister Mackenzie King allowed the execution to proceed in the face of such doubt and the public outcry. Aside from the formal notice denying the appeal for clemency, the Deacon files, comprising three volumes in the Public Archives, give no sign as to why the Governor-in-Council declined to intervene in the carrying out of the death sentence.

Lawrence Deacon was hanged on the tainted evidence of a young woman of questionable morality, who was held as a material witness in the case, and who told a series of conflicting stories both in the courts and in public. Aside from the erratic and changeable evidence of Mrs. Helen Elizabeth Berard, there was little if anything, to connect Deacon to the crime. While police witnesses produced a mass of circumstantial evidence, a Manitoba Court of Appeal judge was to later comment that: "The whole of the so-called circumstantial evidence in the case, in my opinion, in no way contributed to the guilt of the accused, and should not have been put before a jury."

Further, there is the question of a missing witness. Mrs. Yvonne Hamilton, who was living common-law with Deacon at the time of the crime, and who could have substantiated, or destroyed, an alibi put forward by Deacon, was never called to testify. The defence cannot be faulted for failing to call a witness whose evidence might be uncertain, but the failure of the Crown to do so must be considered a breach of the judicial process.

Deacon's final wish that his name be cleared during the lifetime of his mother was not to be. Now, almost 50 years later, the key witnesses have disappeared and cannot (or will not) be traced. There is little likelihood that new light will be shed on the crime, unless this book has that effect. Mrs. Beatrice Deacon, who immigrated to Canada from Bristol, England, with her eight-year-old only child in 1919, died of cancer of the pancreas at the age of 75 in July 1959. She lies alongside her son in St. James Cemetery. The graves share a simple stone bearing only the inscription "Deacon."

Lawrence Deacon spent the last two-and-a-half hours of his life with his former army padre, Reverend J. O. Anderson, who told the press: "We talked about the things a man would discuss with his padre. He told me he was innocent of the murder. He was calm and talked freely, but seemed bitter that he had to die." Several hours earlier, at his last meeting with defence counsel Harry Walsh, Deacon similarly maintained his innocence. Mr. Walsh, who went on to become one of Canada's foremost defence lawyers, recalled that Deacon had to be convinced that an appeal to Ottawa for clemency should be undertaken after the final court appeal was lost: "He said that he had already spent two years in a cell for a crime that he did not commit, and he did not want to spend the rest of his life locked up. He said, 'Let them hang me, and my death will be on their consciences.'"

The two-year ordeal of Lawrence Deacon began on March 31, 1946, in a period when Canada's swollen wartime armed services were being dismantled. All across Canada sailors, soldiers and airmen were still returning home and being posted to discharge units to be processed back to civilian life. That Sunday morning two soldiers, awaiting discharge at Fort Osborne Barracks in Winnipeg's Tuxedo area, braved a misty, freezing drizzle to relieve the boredom of their final days of barracks life. Walking south in a yet to be developed area on Kenaston Boulevard, Private George Goodfellow and Sapper Albert Berg stumbled upon the scene of a murder. At a point some half mile south of Tuxedo Avenue, where the barracks was situated, Goodfellow glanced to the left and noticed an empty taxicab stalled about 70 yards east of the road in a clearing in the bush. Walking in some 40 yards to investigate, the soldiers saw a body lying a short distance from the dark blue cab.

Retracing their steps, Goodfellow and Berg ran back to the barracks and alerted the duty corporal. Within 15 minutes the Royal Canadian Mounted Police were on the scene, followed some ten minutes later by the Winnipeg City Police. Shortly afterwards, about 10 a.m., the provincial coroner, Dr. I.O. Fryer, arrived. They found a grim scene of violence. The taxi was stalled at an angle to the trail in some muddy ruts. The body, lying 18 feet to the north of the cab, was that of 43-year-old Johann Johnson. His head and face had been shattered by vicious blows from a blunt instrument and the skull was broken into small pieces. There were eight deep, jagged lacerations extending from the right cheekbone to the back of the head. The right shoulder and chest were covered with blood and the sleeves of his jacket were hunched up at the shoulders, showing that the body had been dragged by the arms to the spot where it lay face upwards. Both trouser pockets were partly turned out and $1.08 in change lay exposed in the crease of the right hand pocket.

In the right inside pocket of the victim's jacket, police found a wallet containing a registration card, a liquor permit, and $35 in bills. Noting that the body was growing cold, Dr. Fryer estimated that Johnson had met his death about 3 or 4 a.m. that morning. When the body was moved the ground was dry underneath it, although it had been raining. Lying near the body, damp but not wet, was a piece of paper. It was a memorandum from the Department of Veteran's Affairs made out to a discharged soldier, David Schwab of 602 Magnus Avenue in Winnipeg. Strangely, existence of that paper was not revealed at the subsequent inquest, nor at the preliminary hearing on a charge of murder against Deacon. Schwab did not appear as a witness until the first jury trial of Deacon some seven months later.

The inside of the taxi, a 1940 Chrysler sedan, registered in the name of Johnson as an independent owner-operator affiliated with the United Taxi Association, was splattered with gore. There was a large pool of blood on the right side of the front seat; blood on the windshield and on the dashboard as well as on the inside of the right front door and window. When the right front door was opened, police found a large quantity of blood and hair sticking to the running board. Of importance in the later sequence of events, the taxi did not have a light on the roof and the mechanically wound fare meter was attached to the dashboard by a metal bracket, rather than built in.

The evidence was clear. Johnson had been murdered inside the cab, had fallen across the front seat to the right, and had been dragged by the shoulders head first from the car. The car had then been started up and moved some 15 or 16 feet. At that point a left turn had been tried, but the heavy car became stuck in some deeper ruts and was abandoned. Quite clearly, given the charnel-house condition of the car, the person, or persons, who committed the crime would have had their clothes heavily soiled with blood.

To the east of the stalled car, and leading deeper into the bush away from Kenaston, were some "fairly fresh" tracks showing that another car, or truck, had been stuck and that considerable difficulty had been experienced in getting it moved. While Winnipeg police dismissed the finding of these tracks as being immaterial to the case, it should be noted that it had not started to rain until about 1 a.m. that morning. If the trail had been dry before that, there was less likelihood that a vehicle would have become stuck.

As Winnipeg police, aided by about 15 rookie constables in

training, fanned out through the area, further clues were uncovered. In the ditch at Kenaston, where the trail intersected, there were footprints which turned north. Of more significance, a motorcycle constable that afternoon found car tracks on the west side of Kenaston about one-tenth of a mile south of Tuxedo Avenue, and nearly half a mile from where the taxi was found. Close by were some prints leading into the bush on the west side of the road. They appeared to have been made by a woman's shoes. Fourteen feet from the prints was a receipt for $79 made out to Johann Johnson for care of his estranged wife in a mental institution at Selkirk, Manitoba. Almost two weeks later a 15-year-old boy, searching for refundable bottles, found a wallet in the same area. It lay 40 feet west of the shoeprints on the west edge of Kenaston behind a low bush. Inside were papers and documents belonging to Johnson, but no money.

The apparent murder weapon was found on the second day of the search for clues. One of the police recruits found a heavy 18-inch-long bolt lying in a pool of water 70 feet southwest of where Johnson's body had been found. Of a type used in bridge building or railway construction, the bolt was three-quarters of an inch in diameter, weighed two pounds 12 ounces and had a large square nut on one end. The crude weapon was wrapped in several sheets of newspaper tied securely with a white cord. Police Chief George Smith described it as a "weapon that only an amateur type of criminal would use."

One week after discovery of the body, further footprints were discovered one mile south of where the taxi was abandoned in a soft spot in the center of Kenaston Boulevard. From the prints it was deduced that a woman, wearing only one shoe, had been running away from the murder scene toward the sparsely inhabited area lying south of the Canadian National Railway tracks at the end of Kenaston. Nearby in the bush on the west side of the road, a handkerchief bearing the initial "J" was found around the same time.

As police continued to gather clues, Walter Van Walleghem, operator of Royal Dairies at the south end of Cambridge Street near the area where the murder happened, acted on a hunch. He concluded that a person fleeing the crime would head south away from the bright lights and toward some dairy farms lying beyond the railway tracks. On questioning some dairymen and drivers in the district, he was told of the appearance of a distraught and dishevelled woman in the early hours of March 31 at the Winnipeg Dairy on Waverley Street at Parker Avenue, south of the CNR tracks.

Van Walleghem immediately contacted the police and Inspector of Detectives David Nicholson sent two detectives, James Ayres and Albert Manning, to the Winnipeg Dairy which lay roughly a mile south and a mile-and-a-half east of where Johnson's body had been discovered. The dairy owner, Edmund De Backere, told the detectives of the early morning visit. Responding to a knock on his kitchen door at 5:10 a.m. on March 31, he went downstairs with his wife. Opening the door, they found a bedraggled woman, smelling strongly of liquor, standing in the shadows. Her skirt and stockings were covered with mud and she was carrying one shoe. She first enquired if she was on Parker Avenue. Assured that she was, the woman asked directions to 1215 Parker and left.

Even today Parker Avenue is a town planning anomaly, being only half the width of a normal street with a scattering of houses on the south side only. In 1946 the houses were few and far between and separated by bush. It was at 1215 Parker that Ayres and Manning learned the identity of the bedraggled lady. She was 28-year-old Mrs. Helen Elizabeth Berard, who apparently had a wartime relationship with one of the sons living in the Parker Avenue home.

At 4 p.m. on April 9, Nicholson instructed the two burly detectives to pick up Mrs. Berard at 1064 Dudley Avenue, where she and her husband Private Leo Berard and their three children lived in a small, recently built wartime house. Held as a material witness in the murder of Johann Johnson, she was to spend the next month in a dingy upstairs cell in the aging and run-down Central Police Station on Rupert Avenue. Court documents show that she was finally released on bail on surety bonds of $3,000 posted by Steve and David Tanczuk. During her time in custody, Mrs. Berard's tale of the events of the early morning of March 31 was to vary, sometimes dramatically.

A short, attractive brunette, Mrs. Berard had married at the age of 17 during the depths of the Depression in 1935. Early in the Second World War her husband enlisted in the Winnipeg Grenadiers, an infantry regiment. Ill-trained and lacking equipment, the Grenadiers were part of the Canadian reinforcements that arrived in the doomed British Crown Colony of Hong Kong on November 16, 1941. Twenty-two days later the Japanese attacked, and on Christmas Day the governor of the colony surrendered what remained of his garrison. Over one-quarter of the 1,975 Canadian troops were killed, or died in Japanese prisoner of war camps. Leo Berard was one of the survivors.

Thus, at the age of 23, Helen Berard was left alone for nearly five years with three young children. When her husband returned home, after almost four harrowing years as a prisoner, he chose to stay in the army and was stationed at Fort Osborne barracks. That the enforced separation had imposed a strain on the marriage soon became evident. On Saturday night, March 30, 1946, the strains made themselves apparent at a party held to celebrate the Berard's eleventh wedding anniversary. The party at their small home began sometime after 9 p.m. and, with two 24-bottle cases of beer and a 26-ounce bottle of rye whisky available, soon deteriorated into a quarrelsome free-for-all.

The early events of that night are clear. Helen Berard was alone when the first guests, Arthur Munn and his fiancee Margaret Thorburn arrived. They had several drinks before Leo Berard returned home at around 10 p.m. accompanied by Charles

Starkell and his wife Violet. Starkell, a driver for Veteran's Taxi, was on duty and could not stay. Some time after 11 p.m. the final guests arrived. Leo Berard's sister, Mrs. Yvonne Hamilton, arrived with Lawrence Deacon and Mr. and Mrs. Allan Cooper. Shortly after, Deacon and Mrs. Hamilton began to quarrel. They went into a bedroom where Margaret Thorburn, who had become ill, was resting on the bed. When Mrs. Berard went in and tried to pacify them, Leo Berard told her to leave them alone to settle their own disputes and another argument erupted. Despite attempts by Helen Berard and Mrs. Cooper to have him stay, Deacon angrily left the party at around 1 a.m. He returned about 45 minutes later.

Meanwhile, Charles Starkell had returned to pick up his wife. When they left Yvonne Hamilton went with them. On his return, Deacon asked the whereabouts of Mrs. Hamilton. Told that she had left, witnesses said he flew into a rage and declared: "You had better call the police, cause I'm going to kill the bitch for sure." Announcing that he was going home, Deacon went outside. Allan Cooper and Helen Berard followed and persuaded him to return. Cooper then took Deacon into the bedroom and tried to cool him down.

In the front room yet another argument erupted when Helen Berard angered her husband by relating an incident that happened on their first wedding anniversary. Shouting insults she ran out the front door. Allan Cooper and Deacon went outside and brought her back. Ten or 15 minutes later she ran out again. This time Leo Berard and Deacon went out to find her. Berard went two houses east and circled back around the lane while Deacon searched west. When Berard came back to the street, Deacon told him that he had found Helen crouched on her knees hiding against a nearby verandah. After telling her not to be so silly and to get back in the house, Berard asked Deacon to help him, and together they carried her back into the house.

Once inside she rushed into the bedroom, pushed two one

dollar bills down the front of her blouse, put on a brown polo coat and stormed back into the front room. When her husband rose from where he was sitting on the couch, she threw some change from her coat on the floor and screamed: "If it's money you want here it is. I don't want your money." Feeling disgusted, Leo Berard sat down again, and when Deacon saw that her husband would not stop her from leaving, he stood back as well.

The Coopers, Art Munn and Margaret Thorburn had decided to stay the night and Leo Berard urged Deacon to stay as well. However, shortly afterwards, Deacon said that he was feeling alright again and that he was going home to bed. Leo Berard placed the time of Deacon's departure at around 3 a.m. Allan Cooper estimated that Deacon left 1034 Dudley around 3:30 a.m., and said that Helen Berard had left the house some 20 minutes earlier, "about 3 a.m. or shortly afterwards." The events of the rest of the night are not so certain, and the times have some importance in the evidence that would be presented later at the trials of Lawrence Deacon.

These events, backed by all the pertinent witnesses, except Mrs. Hamilton who was never called, are equally significant in light of the contention of the Crown and police that Deacon prepared the murder weapon in his downtown room before attending the party. It is a thesis that obviously does not appear to fit into the sworn testimony of the events leading up to and during the anniversary party.

Chapter Two

Conflicting Statements

Shortly after four o'clock on the afternoon of April 9, detectives James V. Ayres and Albert J. Manning rang the doorbell at 1064 Dudley Avenue and asked Helen Berard to accompany them to the Central Police Station on Rupert Avenue.

Over the next several days she made several statements under close questioning by the police. Those statements while similar in some respects, varied widely in others. She did not consult with a lawyer until over a month later, and would testify that statements implicating Deacon in the murder of Johann Johnson had been made at the insistence of detectives. Those statements, and her evidence at the coroner's inquest, sent Lawrence Deacon to the gallows two years later. Without them the mass of circumstantial evidence presented by the police would have had little relevance.

In the first two statements, made late that afternoon, Helen Berard made no mention of Deacon. The third one, copied down by Detective Ayres, did. In it she gave sketchy details of the anniversary party and of her argument with her husband. She added that, after running outside, Deacon, who she consistently called "Lorne," found her and took her back in the house. She said he told her that, if she did not want to stay, she should go out through the back door and he would meet her on Lorette Avenue, the next street behind the house. After going out the back door, she sat in an outhouse behind a house in construction on Lorette for about 15 minutes, then walked out onto the street. There, she said, she met Deacon. They walked together to Corydon Avenue and Stafford Street where they waited for about 15 minutes for a taxi to come along. One eventually came from the west on Corydon, and Deacon walked out and flagged it down, she said.

"It was a navy blue cab and the meter was on the dash, and I didn't notice the name on it. The driver was a middle-aged fellow, not very big, and his hair was black, but he had a bald spot on the back of his head, and he wore no cap," the statement said. (Johnson's hair was light brown and he did not have a bald spot on the back of his head, according to evidence given by his brother Einar Johnson. Reference to the meter being "on the dash" is open to interpretation, but has some importance in the course of events.)

The statement continued that, when she entered the cab, Deacon got in first and sat on the left side behind the driver. She did not hear Deacon give the driver directions, nor could she remember if the cab went straight ahead or turned around. "Lorne asked me if I knew a bootlegger and I said, "even if I did I wouldn't take you to one at this time of night.' He also said, 'Shall we go to my place,' and I said; 'No, I don't want to run into Yvonne there.' He said, 'Well we can go somewhere else.' I said, 'I wouldn't go, for you are like Yvonne, you would squawk your head off. I wouldn't trust you.' I didn't hear the taxi driver say anything."

Helen Berard added that a quarrel then ensued over her not trusting him, and that she asked the taxi driver to stop and let her out. When they stopped, she said, they were at a set of streetcar tracks turning to the right. After leaving the cab she had run into the bush, circled and came back out onto the road. Eventually, she came to some railway tracks and walked down them to Pembina Highway, said the statement.

Given the fact that Ayres insisted during his testimony that the statement was given without any prompting, or questions being asked, it ended on a strange note: "A week before that

Saturday I was with my girl friend Jean Gauthier, Lorette, Man., and we were downtown, and I had forgotten my hanky, and she gave me an Irish linen hanky with a 'J' in the corner. When I left the taxi Lorne stayed in there and I haven't seen him since."

When Ayres delivered that statement to Inspector Nicholson, he and Manning were instructed to pick up Deacon and bring him to the detective office. Ayres later testified that, when they went to Deacon's small rented room at 159 Donald Street in downtown Winnipeg that Deacon was alone. Manning said Mrs. Hamilton was present. Questioned by Nicholson about 7:45 p.m. in the detective office, Deacon told of attending the Berard's anniversary party, and of his argument with Mrs. Hamilton. He added that he left the party about 3 a.m., and had walked to the corner of Corydon where he got a cab and went home. He estimated his time of arrival at Donald Street as between 4:30 and 4:45 a.m.

Deacon was allowed to leave, but shortly afterwards Nicholson ordered Ayres and Manning to pick him up again. Both agreed that Mrs. Hamilton was present in the room on the second visit. They said that, when Deacon was asked to return to the police station, he said: "You were lucky to catch me. I was just going out to get drunk." Going to a closet which ran down one side of the room, Manning began to inspect the dark blue overcoat that Deacon wore on the night of the party at the Berard's. When Mrs. Hamilton asked what they were looking for, Deacon replied: "I know what he is looking for, but he won't find anything on the coat." While the prosecution was to put heavy emphasis on that statement at the later jury trials, it would seem natural that, after the first visit with Nicholson, Deacon would surely know why he was being interrogated, and what the detectives hoped to find on his coat.

On his return to Nicholson's office, Deacon repeated his earlier statement, adding that he had flagged a seven-passenger cab and had driven straight home to his room and that Mrs.

Hamilton was there when he arrived. She had given him five dollars to go back downstairs and pay the cab driver, he said. Taken into custody about 8:30 that evening, Deacon was held on a coroner's warrant as a material witness in the slaying of Johnson. Three days later, at 2:15 p.m. on April 12, Deacon was charged with murder as a result of further police interrogation of Helen Berard.

After he was formally charged, Nicholson took down another statement, which Deacon refused to sign. It read: "I have told my story and that is the truth. I made a statement that I picked up a seven-passenger taxi—because I saw no name on it and the size at the back would look more than a five-passenger. When I left Berard's home, I walked on Dudley to Stafford, on Stafford to Corydon and east about half a block when a taxi came east on Corydon. I stopped it and got in. I went to my room, saw Mrs. Hamilton who was there and went downstairs and paid the taxi driver."

On the second day of her confinement in the Rupert Avenue Jail, Helen Berard asked for some paper and composed another statement in her own handwriting. The opening part of that statement was almost identical to the one copied down by Ayres on the previous evening. But, when she got to the point where she said an argument broke out between herself and Deacon in the taxi and she had asked the driver to stop, there were some damning additions that would seal the fate of Deacon:

"As he stopped, Lorne said to me 'you're nothing but a whore anyway.' I grabbed the door handle to jump out when I saw Lorne raise his arm up. I was scared and closed the door after me and turned and grabbed the handle. I noticed there was gravel under my feet and looked up in the cab and I didn't see the driver behind the wheel and saw he was lying down on the seat. I yelled, 'Now what the hell have you done?' Lorne answered 'Never mind, take this and beat it.' I ran. I know I threw something soft away in the bush Lorne had given me. I took it with my left hand; it was something soft and a light colour…"

Shortly afterwards she wrote an addition: "I now recall that when Deacon and I got into the taxi at the corner of Corydon and Stafford that we both got in on the right side, and that Deacon got in first and sat down on the left side immediately behind the driver, and when I got in I stumbled on the top step and when my head was down, I saw something lying behind the driver's seat on the floor of the taxi and immediately in front of Deacon's feet. It was a long narrow thing and was wrapped in white paper… I am also sure it was his left arm that was raised when I was getting out of the cab. Lorne Deacon has never called me nor has he talked to me since I left the taxi that night."

That same morning, Nicholson and Manning went to the jailer's quarters at 11 a.m. and asked Helen Berard if she would come with them and point out the route taken by she and Deacon in the taxi. There is no indication that she was given the standard police warning that anything she might say would be taken down and could be used as evidence against her as a material witness, before their departure in a cruiser car. There can, however, be little doubt regarding her state of mind. A small, confused woman, knowing nothing of her legal rights, was confined in a police car with two very big policemen. In the 1940s the requirement that police applicants pass rigid weight and height requirements were still in effect, and only large men were recruited to serve as "Winnipeg's finest."

For a woman who earlier could not remember whether the taxi had gone straight ahead or turned around, Helen Berard was now remembering things in great detail. Taken to the corner of Corydon and Stafford, she traced a route far longer and more complicated than that outlined in her previous statements. After pointing out where she and Deacon got into the cab, she told Manning to drive east in a direction away from the murder scene. The route led downtown to Donald Street and York Avenue, where she pointed out the window in Deacon's room. When they arrived there in the early morning of March 31, she said, the light was on in the window and she figured Mrs. Hamilton was home and that they could not go in.

At her direction the cruiser then drove back to Stafford and Corydon where, she said, Deacon had suggested that they go out to Rosie's place in Charleswood. Rosie was a relative by marriage to Mrs. Berard. The route then led to Academy Road and west to Kenaston Boulevard, where she instructed police to drive south. (Police witnesses never revealed in court that there was no way to reach Charleswood by driving south on Kenaston Boulevard.) It was here, she said, that the quarrel occurred and she decided not to go out to Charleswood. The cruiser was stopped about a tenth-of-a-mile past Tuxedo Avenue. Alighting from the car, Helen Berard pointed out the prints of her shoes in the soft earth on the shoulder of the road. Re-enacting her version of the events, she turned and showed the detectives how she had grasped the handles on the right hand side of the taxi and looked in. When she grasped the handles, she could not see the driver, and looking down she saw him stretched out with his head against the right front door, she said.

The detectives were elated. There had been a similar murder the previous October which stood unsolved. Taxi driver Arthur Badger had been bludgeoned to death in suburban Kirkfield Park and there had been several robberies of taxi drivers in the interim. The Taxicab Association offered substantial rewards for information, and the police department had been under heavy pressure to solve the crimes. They now felt certain the murder of Johann Johnson had been solved. But, as events unfolded over the next two years, many Winnipeggers began to have grave doubts. Over that period, Helen Berard would change and embellish her story in the courts and in public. For the moment, however, it was constant, and the public read the first details when Helen Berard gave evidence at the coroner's inquest held in the grimy courtroom at the Rupert Avenue police station on April 23. Except for a few additions, her evidence was almost identical to her written statement.

With the case producing eight-column headlines on the front pages of the Winnipeg newspapers, interest in the court proceedings was intense. The news coverage became even more sensational when new evidence was presented at the preliminary hearing. Since the coroner's inquest Mr. and Mrs. H.J. Gray, owner's of Gray's Auction Mart in downtown Winnipeg, had retained prominent counsel to defend Deacon. Except for his wartime service with an armoured regiment, the Fort Garry Horse, Deacon had worked for the Grays for ten years. Wounded in the neck in France when American aircraft bombed short of their target, Deacon had returned to work for them after his discharge as a sergeant at war's end. Despite Helen Berard's evidence, the Grays were utterly convinced of his innocence.

When the preliminary hearing to decide if there was enough evidence to commit Deacon for trial on the murder charge opened on June 16 in the same grimy Rupert Avenue courtroom, the Hon. E.J. McMurray, K.C., a former solicitor-general in the federal cabinet, sat at the counsel table. Assisting him as associate defence counsel was Harry Walsh, a young man beginning to make his mark as a criminal defence lawyer. The dignified and eloquent McMurray with a leonine shock of white hair, and the incisive Walsh, who cross-examined with bulldog persistence, made a formidable defence team.

Pressing for the indictment against Deacon was Brigadier O.M.M. Kay, a tall, balding, veteran prosecutor of the hurly-burly legal battles in the magistrates court at the Central Police Station. Presiding over the preliminary hearing was tough-minded Magistrate Maris H. Garton, renowned for running a tight court.

Today the evidence presented at preliminary hearings is seldom privileged to the press. Defence lawyers can, and usually do, request a ban against publication of the evidence. The reason is obvious. Details revealed by the media could jeopardize the fair trial of an accused person by prejudicing potential jurors at the later trial, should the accused be committed. In 1946, however, such evidence was reported at length and in lurid detail. There is no doubt that the sensational press coverage of the inquest and preliminary hearing in the Deacon case influenced the eventual result. A measure of the influence was given in the dramatic reporting in the *Winnipeg Free Press* on the first day of the preliminary hearing. The lead paragraph, spread over three columns on the front page, declared: "A piece of string found in a clothes closet that allegedly matched string used to bind newspaper wrappings on the murder weapon may be the slender clue that will bring a man to the gallows for the slaying of Johann Johnson."

That piece of string was one of 56 exhibits entered into evidence at the preliminary hearing by 32 witnesses. It, like other circumstantial evidence littering the Crown's case, was extremely suspect. The string was put into evidence by Inspector Nicholson, who described having found it on April 11 while searching Deacon's room. The four-and-a-half inch piece of string was found dangling from a nail in the closet. Driven into the wall on the opposite side of the closet was another nail. The length of a string that was required to reach between the two nails would be 36 inches, said Nicholson. There was a kink in the string used to bind the newspaper covering the murder weapon, showing it had been tied around a nail, he said, and that kink was exactly 31 1/2 inches from the end of the string. Comparison of the strings showed that they matched, declared the inspector. (An expert witness from the RCMP Crime Laboratory in Regina later declined to go that far. He would only say that the two pieces of string were "similar," and could come from any number of sources.) The inference in the Crown's case was that Deacon had prepared a weapon before attending the Berard's party with the intent of committing a crime. To support that theory, a plan of the room and closet was entered as an exhibit. (That most improbable likelihood will be examined in detail later.)

The piece of string, however, was not the principal concern of McMurray and Walsh. They would have to discredit the damaging evidence put forward by Helen Berard at the inquest. Foreseeing that evidence, and in the hope of finding chinks and inconsistencies to offset the damage, McMurray might have made a fatal error. He could not have known that she would throw a bombshell into the court by making an unexpected and dramatic change in her story. Cross-examining Detective Manning, in advance of Helen Berard's appearance on the stand, McMurray asked for production of the statements given by Helen Berard during her interrogation in the detective office on the first two days she was held in custody. They were produced and entered as exhibits 16, 17 and 18. When Kay began reading the statements into the record, McMurray rose to object, saying he did not think they would be read until Mrs. Berard had given her evidence. Kay shot back: "My learned friend has filed them. What they contain is now on the record." Magistrate Garton allowed him to continue reading the statements.

Had the damaging statements not been entered at that time, the Crown might have experienced far more difficulty at the coming jury trials in having Mrs. Berard declared as a hostile, or adverse witness. Because the statements became part of the record, it enabled the Crown to launch an intense and searching cross-examination of their own star witness, which might have been denied them otherwise. That turn of events undoubtedly made a strong impact on the minds of the jurors at the trials.

When Helen Berard began her evidence at the preliminary hearing, it opened along the same lines as it had at the coroner's inquest. Making notes at the counsel table, Walsh noted an important variation at the point where she said she and Deacon flagged a taxi on Corydon Avenue. Asked by Kay if she knew what type of car it was, she replied: "No. Just a dark coloured car, but it had lights on top." There followed some minor changes about the discussion in the taxi when it reached Donald Street and then turned back.

Suddenly, major changes in the narrative began to emerge. Describing the decision to go to Rosie's place in Charleswood, Mrs. Berard said the taxi turned off Kenaston onto Tuxedo Avenue and went past Fort Osborne Barracks, continuing to the road where No. 3 Wireless School was situated, before turning back. Shaftesbury Boulevard, on which No. 3 Wireless School was located, lies about a mile further to the south and west of where she earlier said the taxi stopped, and was on the only route to reach Charleswood in 1946. She continued that they came back along Tuxedo Avenue and it was there that she and Deacon had started fighting.

"He was putting his hand under my knee, and I shoved it away. He put it back, and forced it up my skirt, and I shoved him and said 'stop,' and he pulled me back on the seat and held me there, and I hollered to the taxi driver to stop and they stopped and let me out."

Kay was beginning to sense a radical change in the story being told by his chief witness: "At which point?"

"Where Tuxedo starts to turn into Kenaston."

"That's where the streetcar makes the turn from Tuxedo Boulevard to Kenaston?"

"Yes, I got out and the taxi driver said: 'You shouldn't treat her like that when she's tight.'"

"Who did he say that to?"

"Said it to Lorne. Lorne said 'mind your own business,' and he said, 'She won't find her way home,' and I said, 'I've never been lost yet,' and I closed the door and I ran back towards Tuxedo."

"On Tuxedo?"

"On the street there, and I stopped just where the streetcar turns there, and I saw the taxi start up towards Portage."

With the unexpected turn in the evidence, Kay had turned to the counsel table to retrieve the inquest transcript. Visibly startled, he turned back: "What taxi?"

Continuing in a calm, controlled voice, Helen Berard replied: "The taxi I got out of, and I stood there and I started to cry because I didn't know how I was going to get another car to go home. Then I saw a car come back."

"From where?"

"From Portage way. And it went straight over the tracks straight up Kenaston, and I started running. I thought maybe Lorne had come to look for me, and I went up there and I got up to the car and the light was on in the car."

"Where was the car?"

"On Kenaston road."

"How far up the road?"

"It wasn't quite a quarter of a mile. I had come up behind the car, and I put my hands below the back window and I went around to the side of the car and I saw this fellow and I grabbed the handles and looked in."

"What handles?"

"The door handles. I looked up and I saw this fellow in the front seat lying down and I hollered: 'What the hell have you done?'"

"Who did you yell that to?"

"This fellow who was in the back seat."

"Who was in the back seat?"

"I don't know who it was. He had a hat on, and he says; 'Take this and get rid of it,' and he handed me a cloth. I grabbed it with my left hand and I ran."

Mrs. Berard then told of running in a direction away from the streetcar tracks and into the bush. Hearing a noise she stood still in the middle of a bush and saw a man standing on the road. When he turned back to the taxi, she continued her flight through the bush. Stumbling through puddles one of her shoes came off. Picking it up, she went back to the road. On looking back, she saw the car's headlights and fled toward the railway tracks, she said.

Her path then led down the tracks until she reached what she thought was Pembina Highway. There she approached a CNR repair shop and spoke with two young men who brought a small car out of a garage and gave her a lift to Parker Avenue. After making enquiries at the dairy, she made her way to 1215 Parker and called three or four times under the bedroom window of Alex Zrudlo. "I woke Alex up and he said he would be out in a minute, and I went out in the back shed."

When Alex, who she said she had known for four or five years, came out, they went back to the garage behind the house. There she took off her shoes and stockings and Zrudlo went back into the house and got some water for her to wash her feet. He then lit a fire in the garage and the stockings were burned. She did not know what happened to the shoes, and Alex brought her a pair of his sister's shoes, Berard told the court. She stayed in the garage until about noon the next day, then she and Zrudlo went downtown on the streetcar and went to Bill Humicki's place on Spence Street. About a quarter to six, they went to the Spoon Cafe where she had a sandwich. Zrudlo then said he had something to do, and she decided to go home and get her other coat. He loaned her 50 cents for streetcar fare and she went home. Her husband was there when she arrived, she said.

When Kay asked her to go back through the evidence again, McMurray objected that the Crown was leading and cross-examining its own witness. Denied by Magistrate Garton from confronting Helen Berard with her previous statements, Kay tried another tack and zeroed in on the ride she had taken with Nicholson and Manning.

"Where did you show the police officers where you had gone that night?"

"I showed them Stafford and Lorette."

"I am talking about when you got to Kenaston and Tuxedo."

"I stopped them on Kenaston and Tuxedo there and I showed them the road down Kenaston."

"Where on Kenaston?"

Stung by the repeated questioning, Helen Berard suddenly fought back: "Near the barracks. Where I got out there. But, when I got in here and was questioned by Mr. Nicholson this was the first time I had been in court, and I didn't know the procedure. I told them I couldn't remember where I had been. I said 'ask Lorne where we were, ask him,' and they said if you don't tell us we will lock you up: you will stay here. That night until 10 o'clock they were still after me."

"Is that the night you wrote Exhibit 17?"

"I wrote that in the daytime. I told Mr. Nicholson that I had seen a light on the car, and Mr. Nicholson said: 'Oh no you didn't see a light.' Mr. Nicholson also said that, if I changed my statement, I would get from two to ten years."

"When did he tell you that?"

"The day we went out on the road."

Kay ended his examination at that point and the defence took over. With the sudden change in evidence, McMurray kept his cross-examination short:

"You had a good deal to drink that night?"

"Yes sir."

"Did you undergo much examination? I see there are some three or four statements, some in your handwriting. How were these obtained from you?"

"They were obtained by Manning and Nicholson, and if I didn't answer the questions, and I said I didn't know, they said: 'You must know it was Lorne in the taxi. It must have been Lorne in the taxi on Kenaston.'"

"Did you want to make those statements?"

"No I didn't, because I wasn't sure of the story. I knew it couldn't have been Lorne because he didn't wear a hat, and this fellow had a hat."

"You were held prisoner here?"

"Held one month."

"One month in this lockup here?"

"Yes, upstairs."

"And it was during that time you were held a prisoner those statements were made?"

"That's right."

Helen Berard's first ordeal by cross-examination was over. But, the next day, despite an all-out attempt by the defence to break down the evidence, Deacon was committed for jury trial.

Chapter Three

Another Version

The jury trial of Lawrence Deacon at the Fall Assizes of the Manitoba Court of King's Bench in late October was six weeks away when Veteran's Taxi driver Charles Warren swung his cab onto Maryland Street in Winnipeg's west end in the early morning hours of September 16, 1946.

It was close to 4 a.m., and Warren, nearing the end of his shift, hoped the call would be for a short trip. Drawing up in front of one of the tall, narrow, two-and-a-half-storey frame houses that stretch in a dreary line close to the street on the slowly decaying fringe of the city center, he waited for his passenger. The door of the house opened and a woman, smelling strongly of liquor, came out to the taxi. Climbing into the back seat she directed him to an address on Dudley Avenue. Warren was in no mood for conversation and when, half-way down Maryland, the woman leaned forward and querulously asked if he knew who she was, he wearily replied that he did not, and didn't particularly care. Persisting, the woman said she was out of jail on $3,000 bail. When Warren asked what she had done, the reply that she was Helen Berard didn't register.

In the absence of a reply the woman continued: "I'm the chief witness against Deacon."

Turning his head, Warren snapped: "If I'd known that you never would have gotten into this cab. I was a friend of Johann Johnson, and what you've done is pretty cold."

Momentarily sobered, the woman sat back, then declared

that she had changed her mind and didn't want to go home. "Take me out to Parker Avenue in Fort Garry."

As the taxi turned right at the south end of Maryland to cross over the old two-span bridge across the Assiniboine River, the woman blurted: "Lorne Deacon is not guilty. He didn't kill that taxi driver."

"What makes you think that?"

"He wasn't in the taxi that night."

"The police seem to have a fair amount of evidence against him."

"I don't care, I was in the taxi. I had an argument with my husband and I left the house and I was running out on the corner of Stafford and Corydon when that taxi came along. It stopped, and when I got in there was a man in the back with his coat collar turned up and his hat brim down."

As Warren's cab headed out to Pembina Highway, the woman continued to blurt out her story. She said the taxi drove out to Tuxedo where the man told her to get out of the cab. She said she got out and ran, and was circling back to the taxi when she saw a man standing on the road outside the car. The driver of the cab was slumped over, and the man put something in her hand and told her to "beat it." That was where she lost her shoe, she told Warren.

"That's the story I'm going to tell at the trial. That's the evidence."

"You'd better make it good. You've had three or four stories already."

Shortly after the taxi drew up outside 1215 Parker, a full-faced man of medium height came out. The woman asked to see "Joe," but the man replied that Joe was asleep; "and, in any case, he doesn't want to have anything further to do with you." Despite entreaties, the man refused to talk further. Turning to Warren, the woman declared bitterly: "There you are. You give a man everything and then he throws you down."

Rebuffed, the woman then became uncertain where she

wanted to go. Thoroughly fed up and anxious to end his shift, Warren drove her back to the Veteran's Taxi office on Portage Avenue close to Maryland Street where he had first picked her up. There he woke his relief driver, Gerald Nuytten. Pointing to the woman still sitting in the taxi, Warren told him she was alright, but had been drinking: "Take her where she wants to go."

Still drowsy, Nuytten got behind the wheel: "Where to lady?"

"Take me to Parker Avenue in Fort Garry."

Unaware of his partner's experience, Nuytten retraced the route. In the back seat the woman began wailing that nobody knew the trouble she was going through, and started to cry. The performance of the previous drive was repeated: "They say Lorne killed him, but he didn't. Lorne was not in the car at the time."

Back at Parker Avenue, largely the same performance was acted out. This time, however, Joe did come out to the taxi to speak to the woman. She then told Nuytten to drive them out into the bush: "I don't want to be seen talking to this man."

Relieved to get rid of his garrulous fare, Nuytten drove the pair further west on Parker Avenue where he let them out and she paid the fare. As Nuytten drove back downtown, the first rays of sunrise were showing on the eastern horizon.

On the deserted back-road in the dawn, Joe Zrudlo refused to talk. Telling her that he didn't want her walking past his mother's house, he pointed over the railway tracks and across the deserted fields to where her home lay less than a mile to the north, and told her to walk home.

Shortly afterwards, a milkman beginning his morning rounds gave a lift to a bedraggled woman smelling of liquor. He dropped her off at Dudley Avenue where Private Leo Berard and her three children had again been waiting all night for Helen Berard's return home.

(The foregoing incidents were compiled from affidavits sworn to by Charles Warren and Gerald Nuytten, filed in the Manitoba Court of Appeal, and from answers given by Helen Berard at the second trial of Lawrence Deacon.)

Chapter Four

Luck of the Draw

The ornate marble Courtroom One in the Manitoba Law Courts Building was crowded to capacity on October 28, 1946, when Lawrence Deacon went on trial at the Fall Assizes of the Eastern Judicial District. The regular railbirds—pensioners who enliven their retirement by haunting the courtroom at every trial—and the curious, gathered in the expectation of a drama, were not disappointed.

Shortly after the jury had been chosen and the Crown had outlined the evidence it expected to introduce, a new element of mystery was publicly revealed for the first time. Constable James Speed, the first Winnipeg policeman to arrive at the scene of the murder, introduced into evidence the Department of Veteran's Affairs memorandum issued to David Schwab found near the body of Johann Johnson.

Dominating the front page of the *Winnipeg Free Press* that day was the headline: "Mysterious Paper Highlights Testimony." Associate defence counsel Harry Walsh was quick to zero in on the new evidence. When he asked Speed if the memorandum looked as though it could have lain there for some time, the response was that it could have lain there for days. Walsh quickly reminded Speed that he had testified that the paper was damp, but not wet, and that it had been drizzling and wet that morning.

"Why didn't you tell about finding that paper at the preliminary hearing?"

"It slipped my mind, and anyway no one asked me about it."

"Did it slip your memory, or were you told to say nothing about it?"

It was not until the third day of the trial that deputy attorney-general A.A. "Andy" Moffat, acting for the Crown with C.W. Tupper, tried to dispel the mystery surrounding the DVA memorandum. L.J. Perry, occupational counsellor for the DVA, whose name was written on the back of the memorandum, identified it as one he had issued around February 11, to Schwab. Following Perry to the stand, Schwab said the paper was a memo to the Winnipeg Tutorial Institute. He was interested in raising his educational standard, which was grade five, to grade nine, to take a course in automotive engineering. He said he either threw the paper away at the institute, or destroyed it at home. He had never been on Kenaston Boulevard, and did not know where it was. On the night of March 30, he said, he and a friend, Jack Lee, had gone out to Patterson's barn dance by streetcar. Leaving the dance on the northern outskirts of Winnipeg sometime after midnight they went to the Cornwall Hotel, where Schwab's brother was the night clerk.

The Cornwall was one of several aging, run-down hotels facing onto Winnipeg's tough North Main strip; an area where police patrolled in pairs, and where the Salvation Army's Harbour Light gathered in the drunken strays and derelicts and gave them shelter.

Schwab said that, with his brother and his friend, they had gone to the nearby Exchange Cafe some time after 1 a.m. to eat. Returning to the Cornwall Hotel, he and Lee had stayed with his brother until about 8 a.m., he testified. (Einar Johnson had earlier told the court that he had last seen his brother Johann at the Exchange Cafe on the Friday afternoon before his body was found in Tuxedo.)

Walsh's cross-examination revealed that Schwab had been questioned by the police for two or three hours on the morning of April 1, and for another two or three hours that afternoon. He made a statement to police, but had not signed it. (It was never made clear whether the police had finished their investigation of Schwab, or whether the line of enquiry had been ended after the arrest of Helen Berard.) There also appeared to be some confusion over identification of the slip of paper. Schwab denied there had been any writing on the back of the memo given him by DVA, and maintained there was no address of the Winnipeg Tutorial Institute written on it. Also, he said he thought the memo given him had been smaller than the one produced in court. Schwab showed some confusion when asked by Walsh what he had done with the paper.

"Do you remember destroying it?"

"As far as I can remember I destroyed it."

"Then why did you tell my honourable friend that you either destroyed it or threw it away?"

When Schwab hesitated, Walsh asked if he had anything to hide, and turned away ending the cross-examination.

There was also uncertainty over identification of the handkerchief with the initial "J" on it. The man who found the handkerchief on Kenaston Boulevard on April 17, Albert Verbeck, said he handed it to David Mulligan of 1097 Parker Avenue. But, when Mulligan was called to identify the handkerchief entered as an exhibit, he said it was not the one he handed to police.

Deacon was to have little fortune in the luck of the draw of judges asssigned to preside over his trials. On the first occasion Mr. Justice W.J. Major sat in austere and frosty control of the court. A former attorney-general of Manitoba, Major was nearing the end of his judicial career and had a reputation as a harsh trial judge. A slight man in his black robes, he had a thin face that seemed perpetually creased by some dark sorrow. Few people ever remembered him smiling. His conviction that there was no reasonable doubt regarding Deacon's guilt emerged early in the trial.

Helen Berard was called to the stand on the second day of the trial. Repeating the evidence she gave at the preliminary hearing almost word for word she continued to maintain that after she got out of the taxi, it had driven away with Deacon still in it and another car had appeared. When Moffat asked why she had not reported what she took to be a holdup, Berard replied that she had never thought of it. She said she had first heard of the death of Johnson on the Tuesday after it happened, and even then she did not know that the slaying had happened off Kenaston Boulevard.

When McMurray objected to the line of examination as being irrelevant, Moffat responded by asking Major to rule that Helen Berard was a hostile witness. The story she now told was impossible and was at odds with the evidence she had given at the inquest, he said. At that point, Samuel Freedman—later to become chief justice of the Manitoba Court of Appeal—asked protection of the court for his client Helen Berard. Major granted the request with the admonition that such protection could only be offered if a witness told the truth. "If you perjure yourself, the protection will be removed."

The ruling by Major that Helen Berard was a hostile witness opened the way for the prosecution to cross-examine on her previous statements. Hence, the judge ruled that her previous written statements to police could be entered as exhibits. He would deal with the matter of their credibility when making his charge to the jury, he said. A clear sign of how he would deal with that credibility was given when Walsh moved for a directed verdict of acquittal at the end of the Crown's evidence on the fifth day of the trial. With the jury retired, Walsh contended that, leaving aside the statements of Mrs. Berard entered as exhibits, there was no evidence to implicate Deacon in the murder of Johnson. "There may be, my lord, some scintilla of circumstantial evidence, but none that could reasonably establish the guilt of the accused. Every bit of real evidence offered against the accused is actually consistent with his innocence." Contending that Helen Berard's sworn testimony at the trial absolved Deacon, Walsh said there was no other evidence before the court to convict Deacon. Her oral and written statements to police were not evidence. They only went to assessing the credibility of the witness, he said.

Major's reply was caustic: "You are now asking me to pass judgement on the credibility of that witness. There is a statement implicating the accused in her evidence."

"But, under cross-examination, she said those statements were untrue."

"That is for the jury to pass on now."

"Then, my lord, may I state the other proposition. Are you prepared to instruct the jury to accept those statements as evidence?"

His face set and angry, Major snapped: "I am not going to argue with you. I will decide about it when I make my charge to the jury."

Walsh persisted: "It is her sworn testimony; we must accept her evidence as given before your lordship as the truth."

Walsh had lit a fuse. Major closed the exchange with an indication of what was to come: "Is it the truth? Her attitude in the box while I would not say was one of defiance, was one of reluctance. When the Crown was examining her I had to ask her to speak up continually. When she was being cross-examined by the defence, she spoke up without being asked to do so. No. I deny the motion."

Walsh and McMurray exchanged glances. When the jury filed back in, the senior defence counsel rose and announced the defence was not calling any witnesses, a move that gave them the advantage of following the prosecution's address to the jury. Moffat took one hour and fifteen minutes to deliver a methodical review of the evidence. While declaring robbery to be the motive, he placed his emphasis on Helen Berard's statements to police. McMurray, in his hour-and-a-half summation, stressed that none of the statements by Berard implicating Deacon had been sworn or given under oath. "They were given under police intimidation," he charged.

At 10 a.m. the next day, on the sixth day of the trial, Major delivered a tough one-hour-and-twenty-minute charge to the jury. He began by emphasizing the basic principle of Canadian law that the onus was on the Crown to prove the guilt of the accused. "There is no onus on the defence to prove innocence. Whenever a reasonable doubt exists about the guilt of the accused, the benefit of that doubt must go to the accused." Having made that point, Major then proceeded to make it abundantly clear to the jury that, in his mind at least, there was no reasonable doubt regarding Deacon's guilt. Mrs. Berard's statements to police were not only accepted as evidence; the judge recommended them to the jury as the truth. Her story given from the witness box was "garbled and contradictory," said Major. "The witness has made many statements in this case which, in my opinion, are wholly contradiction of the facts."

There was more to follow. After reviewing her evidence in detail, Major concluded: "My reason for allowing the Crown to cross-examine her on the statements was that I had seen fit to declare her a hostile witness, and I allowed the Crown to so examine to test her credibility. Subsequent developments, in my opinion, prove I was correct in declaring her a hostile witness. Her answers to Crown counsel would indicate, in my mind that the written statement she gave to the police is the true account of what happened that morning. As to her subsequent statements, they constitute one of the most remarkable exhibitions of mental gymnastics ever displayed in a court of law or elsewhere."

The jury retired at 11:10 a.m. with a hanging charge imbedded in its collective mind. Dismayed at the ferocity of the judge's charge, Walsh rose and requested that they be brought back and reinstructed on some of the more damaging points. Major declined. Shortly afterwards, the sheriff's officers escorted the all-male jury—four farmers, two carpenters, two labourers, an engraver, a butcher, a shipper and a mechanic—to a nearby hotel for lunch. Not long after they returned to the jury room the foreman knocked on the door, indicating that a verdict had been reached. In light of the judge's charge, there had not been much need for discussion. When the jury filed back into the courtroom at 2:40 p.m., the outcome was clear. Looking straight ahead, they were studiously avoiding the anxious eyes of Deacon sitting in the marble prisoner's dock facing them.

The clerk of the court rose: "Gentlemen of the jury; have you reached a verdict, and if so, who shall speak for you?" Rising, the foreman said quietly, "Guilty my lord." When Walsh asked that the jury be polled, each rose in turn and confirmed the verdict. Major shifted his gaze to the prisoner: "Lawrence Deacon, you have heard the verdict of the jury, Is there anything you wish to say before I pass sentence?"

Deacon, a slim figure against the high marble backing that screened him from the public section of the court, stood and answered calmly: "I am innocent my lord."

Reaching forward, Major picked up a black cloth from the bench and placed it on his head:

> The sentence of the court is that you be taken to the gaol of the Eastern Judicial District at Headingley in Manitoba, and that you be there confined as the law requires until Thursday, the sixteenth day of January, 1947, and on that day, between the hours of one-o-clock and six-o-clock in the morning, you be taken from your place of confinement to the place of execution and you be there and then hanged by the neck until you are dead; and may God have mercy on your soul.

Deacon took the sentence without flinching, but behind him in the crowded and hushed courtroom his mother began to moan softly. Ashen-faced, Deacon's employer, Mrs. Gray, who had sat with Mrs. Deacon throughout the six days of the trial, reached out to comfort her.

Within minutes of the court being cleared, Harry Walsh told reporters that the verdict would be appealed. The appeal, he said, would be based primarily on the judge's charge to the jury. Even without having the transcript for examination, it was evident there were adequate grounds in that charge on which to base an appeal.

Based on 36 points of contention, the appeal was filed on November 14, 1946, and hearings began in the Manitoba Court of Appeal on Tuesday, January 7, 1947. Since the five-man appeal court was then short two judges, two puisne judges of the Court of King's Bench were elevated temporarily to constitute a full court. Sitting with Chief Justice E.A. McPherson and Justices H.A. Bergman and S.E. Richards of the appeal court were J.E. Adamson and W.J. Donovan.

Carrying the defence argument in the small third-floor appeal court, Harry Walsh encountered early difficulties. He had been arguing his first points for about half an hour when Mr. Justice Richards, who was in advanced years, suddenly looked up from his notes. In apparent confusion, he enquired: "Young man, are you appearing for the Crown or for the defence?" It was scarcely encouragement to a young lawyer arguing his first capital case before the appeal court.

After three days of hearings it became clear that success or failure of the appeal hinged on the eligibility of Mrs. Berard's earlier statements to police as exhibits, and decision was reserved by the court. However, two of the judges had pointedly referred to the fact that McMurray had been the first to cross-examine on the statements given to the police. "You don't subscribe to the trial judge's point that it was the defence who first examined on Exhibit 14 (Mrs. Berard's second statement to police, in which she implicated Deacon.) and it was the defence; therefore, who allowed it in?" asked Bergman. Adamson similarly pointed out that McMurray had cross-examined on the written statement. He agreed with Walsh that it had not been for the purpose of discrediting the witness, but added: "That is just the point. Mr. McMurray drew out only points favourable to his client, and therefore, the whole statement was properly entered in evidence."

One week after the appeal hearing, defence counsel were approached by the two taxi drivers, Charles Warren and Gerald Nuytten. They outlined the events of September 16, when Helen Berard rode in their cab. Walsh immediately filed affidavits signed by the two men with the appeal court, and made application for the appeal judges to hear the new evidence.

On January 21, the appeal court turned thumbs down on the application in a four-to-one decision. W.J. Donovan, one of the King's Bench judges, was the sole dissenter. Donovan reasoned that inclusion of the new evidence, volunteered by two independent citizens, would bring two more conflicting stories made by Mrs. Berard before the court. But, he said that should not rule against their acceptance. The whole of the so-called circumstantial evidence in the case, in his opinion, in no way contributed to the guilt of the accused and should not have been put before a jury, said Donovan. As for the new evidence, if the undisputed statements of the two taxi drivers were put before the court, it would give the defence the opportunity to cross-examine Helen Berard on their content. Such cross-examination, along with the evidence before the courts, might lead to the conclusion that Mrs. Berard was of very weak or unsound mind, and might thus have a material bearing on the court's decision on Deacon's appeal, said Donovan.

Given that reasoning, it was not unexpected that Donovan was one of the two judges to dissent when Deacon's appeal was dismissed by a three-to-two decision on February 17. While Chief Justice McPherson and his two fellow appeal court judges, Bergman and the ageing Richards, ruled for dismissal of the appeal, Donovan said he would have granted the appeal and set

Deacon free. His fellow judge on the lower court while dissenting, would not have gone that far. Adamson would have ordered a new trial.

As before, Walsh immediately announced the decision would be appealed. The dissenting judgements allowed him to proceed to the Supreme Court in Ottawa. Had the decision been unanimous, no further appeal would have been allowed. Meanwhile, the first execution date set for January 16, had been deferred to February 27. It was now postponed to June 16, to allow time for the case to be heard by the Supreme Court. On May 15, after three-and-a-half days of hearings before the six red-robed justices of the Supreme Court, Chief Justice Thibodeau Rinfret announced that judgement would be reserved.

One week before the re-scheduled execution date of June 16, Deacon was taken from the condemned cell and again lodged in one of the remand cells at Headingley Jail. The six justices of the Supreme Court had been unanimous in their decision. It was read by Chief Justice Rinfret on June 9, 1947: "The appeal is allowed, the conviction set aside, and a new trial ordered." The Supreme Court ruled that Major had erred in admitting the written statement, given by Helen Berard to police, with a supporting sketch, as evidence at the trial. Mr. Justice Kerwin wrote… "While the actions of counsel for the accused had the effect of making the writing, as well as the sketch, an exhibit, neither could serve as evidence against the accused except, of course, insofar as the witness adopted them as part of her testimony at the trial."

The irascible Mr. Justice W.J. Major might have been seeking a measure of revenge for the reversal in the Supreme Court in an abrasive confrontation with Harry Walsh at the arraignment of prisoners facing trial at the Fall Assizes which opened on October 21, 1947. Presiding over the arraignment, Major set the opening of Deacon's second trial for October 27. Meanwhile, Walsh had been retained to defend another accused murderer, Michael Angelo Vescio, who also appeared at the arraignment. Preliminary hearing on the evidence against Vescio for the shooting of two 13-year-old boys in separate incidents had ended just four days before the arraignment. Faced with a strenuous court battle to defend Deacon, Walsh requested a postponement of the Vescio case to the Spring Assizes. Major refused to grant the traverse, and when Walsh told the court he would be forced to retire from the Vescio case for lack of time to prepare the defence, Major questioned his right to withdraw. His face set and unsmiling, he ventured that Walsh was making "an idle threat."

Fighting to maintain his composure, Walsh assured the court that it was his duty to retire if he could not present an adequate defence. "I presume you will return your retainer," said Major acidly. Walsh assured him the retainer would be returned to the Vescio family. With Walsh remaining adamant, Major set the trial of Vescio for November 10, and appointed a new counsel, John L. Ross, to defend him. (The outcome of that case, one of the most sensational in Winnipeg history, will be dealt with shortly.)

Deacon's ill fortune in the assignment of judges to preside at his trials continued. E.K. Williams, a punctilious enforcer of courtroom decorum who had been appointed chief justice of the Court of King's Bench a short time before, occupied the bench when Deacon's second trial opened. Over the next four years, five men appeared before Chief Justice Williams charged with murder. Not one of them escaped the noose.

One of the first actions taken by Williams upon his appointment as chief justice was to bring back the traditional robes worn by English judges since the reign of Henry VI in the fifteenth century. For years all the judiciary in Manitoba, from county court to justices of the appeal court, had worn black robes along with stiff wing collars and white ties identical to those of the lawyers appearing before them. That did not fit with the new chief justice's sense of decorum. The black robes for the Court of King's Bench (now Queen's Bench) were replaced by a close-fitting violet robe worn with a long black stole. A four-inch wide red sash, known as the "gun case," was attached to the right shoulder and crossed the chest diagonally to be fastened at the left side by a broad, black silk girdle.

Introducing the restored robes to the press, Williams stressed that many persons appearing in criminal court were from Central Europe where such pomp was understood. The robes, he said, would impress upon them the solemnity and majesty of the law. One got the feeling that, if he could have done so without arousing too much of a furore, E.K. Williams might also have adopted the white wigs of the English courts.

Although a slight figure, Williams projected an impressive image. Beneath a crown of white hair, his lean face terminated in a small, neatly groomed goatee, and a pair of glittering blue eyes gave notice that he would tolerate no questioning of his rulings.

When Helen Berard, who had moved to Calgary with her husband, took the stand at the renewed trial, another trial-within-a-trial in the absence of the jury took place. McMurray, foreseeing that she might again be declared a hostile witness, sought a ruling from the chief justice on the admissibility of her statements to police. Williams ruled that he would not make a decision in advance of the situation arising. Shortly afterwards, when Helen Berard again insisted that a second car had appeared after the one bearing Deacon had left the scene, Moffat again asked that she be declared hostile. Williams complied, and ruled that she could not be given the protection of the court against the possibility of a charge of perjury.

With the Supreme Court ruling in mind, the Crown followed a different strategy from that of the first trial. Instead of filing her written statements to police as exhibits, Moffat read them and her evidence at the preliminary hearing to Mrs. Berard. He then cross-examined in detail regarding the truth of the particulars. Coming close to tears under the lengthy cross-examination by the Crown, Helen Berard first declared that some details were true, then withdrew them. Asked by the defence to describe the man she saw in the car with his arm raised; she said the man's face wasn't fat and it wasn't thin, he had on a gray hat and a dark coat. She had not seen the man anywhere else that night, but he looked something like David Schwab who she had seen at the first trial, because Schwab had a gray hat and a dark coat.

When McMurray questioned her on the statements she allegedly made to the two taxi drivers, Charles Warren and Gerald Nuytten, Helen Berard said she had been drinking quite a lot that night and could not remember what she had told them. She had gone to the Zrudlo home to see if Joe Zrudlo would go back to a party on Maryland Street, she said.

Alex Zrudlo followed Berard to the stand. This time he was closely cross-examined by Walsh on his association with the Crown's chief witness. Admitting that he had visited her at several places where she lived during the war, he denied that he had ever continuously lived with her. Shown the bolt used in the murder, he said it might have come off a bridge or could have been used in railway construction. They demolished railway cars near his home, he said, and there were tool boxes in his garage that had similar bolts in them.

When Inspector Nicholson took the stand and revealed for the first time that he had gone to Parker Avenue on April 8, to talk with Alex Zrudlo, McMurray asked why he had not mentioned it at the preliminary hearing or at the first trial. Nicholson replied that no one had asked him. Asked if he had checked up on Zrudlo, Nicholson said he had, but admitted that he had not made an investigation of his shoes or clothes. There had been no search made of the area on Parker Avenue except in the garage. He had seen no bolts of the type on exhibit in the court, said Nicholson, and if he had found any in the garage he would not have thought they were significant. Despite this, when McMurray suggested the investigation had been very superficial, Nicholson denied it.

Even stranger was the evidence produced about the clothing

found in Deacon's room. While detectives made a point of finding a dry cleaner's label in one of the suits, it was not disclosed until Nicholson was asked to produce the date of the cleaning that it was not the suit that Deacon had worn on the night of the party at the Berard's. Further, when Nicholson checked back and returned to the stand the next day, he reported that the date of the cleaning was January 29, 1946, two months before Johnson was murdered.

Nicholson also revealed that David Schwab had been thoroughly investigated and his house and clothing searched. He attached no importance to the fact that Schwab's shoes might have fitted the footprints found around the murder area. "There are thousands of shoes of that type," said the inspector. "That's just the point I'm trying to make," replied McMurray.

At the end of the Crown's case, Walsh again sought a directed verdict of acquittal: "I submit that the evidence of Mrs. Berard is of a dubious nature, and it is with respect m'lord that I submit it is the duty of the trial judge to direct the jury to bring in a verdict of acquittal." Rejecting the motion, Williams said he had spent the weekend reviewing the transcript of the first trial and the legal precedents in expectation of the defence motion. His assessment of the review was ominous: "I have come to the conclusion that the evidence in this case is as strong, or stronger, than the first case."

Summing up for the prosecution, Moffat again stressed the written statements given police by Helen Berard, particularly that part implicating Deacon as the man she had seen with his arm raised in the taxi. "There was no strange car, no strange man; only Deacon there with her." The motive, said Moffat, was robbery.

Anticipating a tough charge from the chief justice, McMurray followed with a lengthy summation to the jury. Pulling out all stops, McMurray castigated Helen Berard as "a liar and a prodigious one." Declaring that none of her evidence could be believed, he added: "The Crown has no more right to hand you evidence from a poisoned, foul source than it has to offer you a drink from a poisoned well." While he did not believe the police had fabricated the story told in her statement, they had fooled themselves. "They got hold of this drunken, frightened, debauched woman and scared the wits out of her."

On Tuesday, November 4, at 10 a.m., Williams began his charge to the jury. Before he finished two hours later, Deacon's fate had obviously been sealed. With the ruling of the Supreme Court in mind, the chief justice went even further than called for in warning the jury about accepting Helen Berard's previous statements as evidence. Directing the jury to accept only part of Helen Berard's evidence, Williams told them to put all the rest of the statements out of their minds. "I direct you to accept only part of the statement that she made at the inquest. In order that there shall be no doubt in your minds, I shall read the portions which are actual evidence against the accused." Reading out the statements by Mrs. Berard at the inquest and to Nicholson, the chief justice stopped at the point where she said she got out of the taxi on Kenaston Boulevard. He then told the jury to ignore all the rest of the statements dealing with the scene of the crime. "You must disregard her story as to what happened after she left the taxi—what happened up to that time, I suggest, is substantially true."

Having made that bow to the ruling of the Supreme Court, Williams gave a pull on the noose: "I suggest to you that both she and Deacon were in the deceased's taxi that night…the second part of the story is incredible, but it is up to you to decide."

Weighing the evidence, the chief justice said he thought it was probable that the murder was committed inside the taxi at the point where it was found. (That conflicted with the clear evidence that Mrs. Berard got out of the taxi almost half-a-mile away as shown by her footprints, in which case she could not have seen Johnson being struck.) Then, in direct conflict with the motive put forward by the Crown, he said the body must have been removed by someone and that, as the wallet and money were still on the body, robbery was not the motive. (That suggestion obviously overlooked the second wallet found on the west side of Kenaston half-a-mile north of where the body was found.)

The lengthy charge, in which Williams told the jury they could bring in only one of two verdicts, guilty or not guilty of murder, was marked by a number of other damaging statements. Dealing with Deacon's statement to Nicholson, the chief justice pointed out the long time lag between the time he said he left the party and the time he arrived home. He also noted that Deacon had said he caught a seven-passenger taxi, and said it was peculiar that the driver had not come forward. He added that: "Mrs. Berard's story placed both her and the accused in the Kenaston Boulevard area in a taxi within half-a-mile of the murder area at a time which the murder was committed. If you believe Deacon's story, then he did not commit the crime and he has established an alibi."

Returning to the motive, Williams told the jury to: "Consider what moved the murderer to kill Johnson. It might be due to remonstrations of the deceased that Deacon, in a rage, attacked Johnson and brutally slew him. That is for you to consider." In other equally damaging references, the chief justice suggested that the jury could assume the taxi caught by Deacon and Mrs. Berard did not have a light on top, and that the murder weapon could readily have been carried on his person by the accused on the night of the slaying. (That unlikely premise will be examined at length later.)

When the jury retired at noon, both Moffat and Walsh requested that they be brought back and reinstructed on several points. Williams icily informed them that he had carefully considered all the points. The jury would not be called back, and the court adjourned at 12:30 p.m. for lunch. Eleven minutes after the court re-convened at 2 p.m., the jury indicated that they had reached a verdict. If any of the jurors had any reasonable doubts regarding Deacon's guilt, the final submission of E.K. Williams had obviously dispelled them. As in the first trial the jury filed back studiously avoiding the anxious eyes of Deacon. The verdict was guilty, and so said they all.

The prisoner being told to rise, and the ritual question addressed to him, Deacon again said: "I am innocent my lord." Williams reached for the black cloth, placed it on his head, and sentenced Deacon to be hanged on January 21, 1948.

Three weeks later, on Tuesday November 25, Chief Justice Williams again placed the black cloth on his head and sentenced Michael Angelo Vescio to be hanged on February 18, 1948. A jury had taken only thirty-five minutes of deliberation to find Vescio guilty of murder.

Walsh filed an appeal against Deacon's conviction on December 2, citing 48 points dealing primarily with the evidence of Helen Berard and Chief Justice Williams' charge to the jury. On January 8, Chief Justice E.A. McPherson of the Manitoba Court of Appeal, granted a stay of execution to March 15, allowing time for the appeal to be presented. The appeal hearing was delayed when Moffat became ill, and a further stay was granted to April 16. One month before that date, on March 15, Chief Justice McPherson read his written decision dismissing the appeal. It was concurred in by Justices S.E. Richards, J.B. Coyne and A.M. Campbell. The fifth judge, A.K. Dysart, read a separate lengthy judgement.

The defence had pinned their hopes on a dissent from Dysart, who had indicated to Walsh earlier that he would rule for a new trial. But, it was not to be. While citing some differences with the majority judgement, Dysart dismissed the appeal. As noted, the rules of the period called for at least one dissent before an appeal could be carried to the Supreme Court. Any hope of saving Deacon now lay in a plea to the federal cabinet for clemency, and substitution of the death penalty with life imprisonment.

Worn out and disillusioned by the tenuous hopes of acquittal being constantly dashed over almost two years of court battles,

Deacon first resisted any application for clemency, preferring the noose to life behind bars. His defence counsel and Lt. Col. Gordon Churchill, who headed an active defence fund committee, persuaded him however, that the final appeal should be undertaken. Churchill, who had served in the same armoured regiment with Deacon, had been elected as one of the three armed services members to sit in the Legislature to represent the interest of the navy, army and air force veterans in the immediate aftermath of the war. He was later elected to Parliament and served as minister of trade and commerce and defence minister in the federal cabinet of Prime Minister John Diefenbaker.

With public sentiment deeply aroused over the sentencing of Deacon, almost solely on the evidence of a single dissolute and unreliable witness, the Deacon Defence Committee had little difficulty in circulating petitions calling for clemency. Young lawyers and law students, appalled at what they perceived as a miscarriage of justice, solicited signatures in downtown restaurants during lunch hours, and members of the legislature joined in the drive. Day after day, Deacon's elderly mother walked from door to door in the residential areas, seeking signatures without revealing her identity. Tired, but still clinging to hope, she returned late each evening to her third floor rooms in a house in the west end of Winnipeg. As the execution date grew nearer, petitions bearing over 10,000 signatures had been sent to Justice Minister J.L. Ilsley in Ottawa. Lawyers and legislators had joined in the clamour for leniency and, with only one week left, the drive for a reprieve was gaining momentum.

But, obviously counteracting that mass outcry was a singularly inept report to the minister from a detached and uncaring bureaucracy in the capital city. Given the facts of the case, the condensed summary and recommendation that went forward to the minister from his department are almost inconceivable when read today. Prepared by a junior civil servant, identified only by his initials, for the deputy minister of justice, the document is callous in its obvious lack of research or appreciation that a man's life was at stake. The document respectfully submitted: "Considering the facts and circumstances of this case, the undersigned is of the opinion the law may well be allowed to take its course."

Those "facts and circumstances," as outlined in a two-and-a-half page summary, might best serve as a lesson in accenting the negative. After stating that reports indicated that Deacon was a married man, who was for some time separated from his wife and three children living in Toronto (if true, this was not shown at any time during the trials.) The summary added that Winnipeg City Police reports disclosed that the accused was living with one Mrs. Yvonne Hamilton as common-law man and wife. That might raise few eyebrows today, but in 1948 it was a damning indictment of moral turpitude. Further, Justice Minister Ilsley, while a brilliant man, was known as a stern moralist who had been described as having the "demeanour of a Baptist Sunday school teacher."

To add insult to that injury, the summary went on to state: "This [Winnipeg police] report also refers to Deacon as a man with a very violent temper, who would always grab a weapon in preference to using his fists. It would appear from the evidence that this crime was committed as the result of an argument, and the attack was made in a fit of temper."

It seems almost inconceivable that the report forwarded to Ottawa by the police should contain such hearsay statements, none of which had been entered as evidence at the trials. Deacon had no previous criminal record to show such behaviour, and his military record would not bear out such allegations. Further, his employers of ten years, Mr. and Mrs. H.J. Gray, completely refuted such behaviour.

After noting that Deacon had told police that he left the Berard home around 3 a.m. and arrived home about 4:30 a.m., the summary stated: "The district where he hailed this taxi was in the vicinity of where the crime was committed. The evidence shows that he could have travelled from Berard's home to his own home in 26 minutes over the route he says he took." The facts are that the place where he hailed the taxi was several miles from where the crime was committed. Also, considerable drinking had taken place at the Berard's party and the evidence of times when events happened were sometimes vague. One witness said Deacon left at 3:30 a.m. His own statement was unclear how long he waited till a taxi came.

While not particularly damaging, the following quote shows the inept nature of the summary submitted to the minister: "Expert medical testimony revealed that death had occurred some six to eight hours previous to 9 a.m., and was the result of a fractured skull, with lacerations and haemorrhage of the brain." Had that been true, it would have placed the death between 1 a.m. and 3 a.m., and ruled in Deacon's favour. The facts are that the coroner arrived on the scene about 10 a.m. and made the estimate at around 10.30 a.m., placing the death of Johnson between 2:30 to 4:30 a.m.

Then, in two short paragraphs on the second page, the remote and disinterested civil servant hammered three or four more very crooked nails into Deacon's coffin. He wrote:

"The police found a stained and muddy handkerchief in the clothes closet of the room occupied by the accused. Expert evidence indicated that the soil found on the handkerchief was similar to the soil taken from near where the taxi was found. The stains gave a positive reaction of blood.

"Casts of footprints found near the taxi were taken, and it was stated that the shoes worn by Deacon could have made some of these prints."

Again, an interpretation that totally distorted the actual evidence. Staff Sergeant J.I. Mallow, an expert witness from the RCMP crime laboratory in Regina, said on the stand that thousands of shoes could have made the imprints, including those of Schwab, whose shoes had plates on them and were size 8.

Deacon's shoes were also size 8, but had no plates such as those recorded at the scene. Mallow also said that stains found on the handkerchief might, or might not have been blood. There was no "positive reaction" of blood. Mallow also said that he could not say there was not other soil, similar to that on the handkerchief, in other areas of Winnipeg. He was not surprised that soil taken on the trail leading to the scene and that near the cab were of different composition.

On the final half-page of the summary it declared: "String taken from the clothes closet in Deacon's room was tested and compared to the string which was wound around the newspaper covering the murder weapon. This was found to be similar in construction and in fibre." A true, but misleading, piece of information gratuitously thrown into the document for the minister. Sergeant James Robinson, of the RCMP crime laboratory, said it was a common piece of string, and he could not say if the two pieces of string entered as evidence came from the same ball or not. He added that a kink in the string did not necessarily point to the fact that it had been tied around a nail, as contended by Winnipeg police witnesses.

Following that summary was 15 pages of comments copied word for word from the report of the second trial submitted by Chief Justice Williams. The summation by the trial judge ended with the general comment:

"The accused was ably defended and his counsel made the most of their opportunity to discount the Crown's witnesses. I believe however, that the failure of the accused to testify, the failure of the defence to produce any evidence to support his alibi, his statement that he could not remember where he had been and the evidence as to his 'furious' behaviour when he found Yvonne Hamilton had left the party, the fact—which was stressed by defence counsel—that the injuries which killed Johnson must have been inflicted by a person who had a deep-rooted grudge against the deceased, or a violent temper, and the accused's statement to Hamilton when referring to his overcoat—he said, 'I know what he is looking for, but he won't find it on the coat'— played an important part in the jury's finding. The jury was an exceptionally good one."

In that brief summation, Williams may have clearly stated his own conviction that Deacon was guilty, and to have avoided showing judicial prejudice by cloaking it as the collective opinion of the jury. If that is the case, then the impression might clearly have been left with the federal cabinet that Deacon's guilt had been established by his failure to testify, and by the failure of his counsel to call witnesses to support the statement he had given to police. In short, the onus was on the accused to prove his innocence; a point which offends against the most fundamental principle of the common law.

The question must now be asked; what evidence could have been produced to support Deacon's statement? Crown counsel and the trial judge made pointed reference to the fact that the driver of the taxi that Deacon said he had taken had not come forward. That does not prove that the driver did not exist. Witnesses are often reluctant to come forward for various reasons. There was another very pertinent and vital witness readily at hand who could have proved or disproved Deacon's innocence. Mrs. Yvonne Hamilton was the only person at the anniversary party at the Berard's who was not called as a witness at any time. The onus was not on the defence to call her. That onus rested clearly on the prosecution.

It is now time to examine that, and other aspects of the case more fully. Was Deacon guilty: or was an innocent man hanged?

Chapter Five

If He's Got to Go, He's Got to Go

Instead of drawing the attention of Justice Minister J.L. Ilsley to the statement allegedly made by Deacon when referring to his overcoat: "I know what he's looking for, but he won't find it on the coat," it would have been more appropriate and pertinent for Chief Justice Williams to have examined the question from Yvonne Hamilton that evoked that response. Therein might have lain the truth of the matter.

When detective Alfred Manning took Deacon's blue overcoat from the closet in their small room at 159 Donald Street on April 9, why did Mrs. Hamilton ask what they were looking for? As earlier noted, Deacon's reply was not unusual. It was the second time that evening that he had been asked to go to the police station. Having been asked on the first occasion about the party at the Berard's, he would probably have phoned the Berard home and found that she was being held as a material witness in the murder of Johann Johnson. It was Mrs. Hamilton's question that was unusual and highly pertinent.

Dr. O.C. Trainor, pathologist at the Winnipeg General Hospital, told the court that anyone who had entered the taxi after Johann Johnson was slain would have had their clothing covered with blood. After describing the multiple injuries to the murdered man's head, he testified that an artery had been severed, and that such an injury would cause blood to "spurt up several feet." On the night of the Berard's party, Deacon was wearing a dark blue, pin-stripe suit, and when he left the party he put on the dark blue overcoat found in his closet. If he killed Johann Johnson that coat and suit would have been covered in blood, as would his hands and possibly his face. The inside of Johnson's cab resembled a slaughterhouse.

Recall that Deacon's statement was that, after coming home, he had gone upstairs to his room. There, according to one statement to Nicholson, he got $5 from Mrs. Hamilton and went back downstairs to pay the cab driver. Did he, or did he not? Only Mrs. Hamilton could have answered that question. If she acknowledged that he did, then the next question would be: "What was the condition of his clothes?" To argue that Mrs. Hamilton might have lied to protect the man she was living with is to avoid the issue. The Crown was duty bound to call her as a witness. It was essential that the jury hear her, and it was the duty of the trial judges to have asked why she was not brought to the witness stand at either of the two trials.

The question can equally be posed whether Mrs. Hamilton could fail to notice the inevitable bloodstains in any event. The room which she and Deacon shared was very small, no more than ten feet by twelve feet at best. A common clothes closet ran the length of one side of that room. Heavy bloodstains could not have gone unnoticed over that late March weekend. If that is accepted, then Mrs. Hamilton's apparent ignorance of why they were examining the coat would show that Deacon was not lying. Clearly too, Yvonne Hamilton could probably have testified as to whether or not Deacon had taken the suit and overcoat out to be dry-cleaned. Surely the police asked her? If they did not, they were either obtuse or derelict in their duty. What did she tell them? If she did tell them something, clearly it was not incriminating. The detectives quoted every innuendo that might be damaging to the accused. Is that why the prosecution neglected the duty of the Crown to call her as a witness?

The point goes further. The detectives gave detailed accounts of the condition of all Deacon's clothing, including the gratuitous and totally extraneous fact that one of the suits bore a dry-cleaning tag. Cross-examination later revealed that it was not the suit worn by Deacon on the night of the Berard party, and that it had been cleaned some months before the murder took place. There was a dry-cleaning outlet a short distance from Deacon's room. Given the spurious emphasis placed on the one suit, why did the police not check there to find if a blue overcoat or blue, pin-stripe suit with massive bloodstains had been dry-cleaned over the previous week. Such clothing would not have gone unnoticed at that, or any other, dry cleaning outlet. Yet no such evidence was produced. Only statements that the clothing was "very clean." Not unusual, since press pictures at the time show that Deacon was a fastidious dresser.

In the same vein, production of a soiled handkerchief and an undershirt with stains that "might have been blood" as exhibits could be regarded as laughable had the circumstances not been so tragic. If Helen Berard's written and oral statements to police, that Deacon was the man she saw in the back seat of the taxi with his arm upraised and driver slumped on the rear seat, were true— and the juries and judges at both trials believed that it was—then he drove that taxi half-a-mile up Kenaston and into the bush with a battered corpse sprawled spouting blood on the front seat alongside him.

Pointing up the ambiguity raised by Helen Berard's statements incriminating Deacon, was the fact that Chief Justice Williams, in his summation to the jury, declared that the murder must have taken place at the spot where the body was found. Granted that may, or may not, have been true. There is, however, clear and uncontroverted Crown evidence that Mrs. Berard got out of a car at a point almost half-a-mile north of where the abandoned cab was found. Her fooprints, leading away from the tire marks on the west side of Kenaston and into the bush were identified and casts taken by the police and entered as exhibits in the court. If, as Williams contended, the murder happened in the clearing to the south, then Helen Berard did not see it happen.

Yet something clearly did happen where her footprints were found. The second wallet and personal papers belonging to Johnson were found near those footprints. The wallet was lying 40 feet to the west in a small clear space behind a bush. How did it get there? While not impossible, it would be difficult to throw a light wallet, with only a few identification papers in it, a distance of 40 feet and have it drop behind a bush. Did Helen Berard drop it in her flight from something, or someone?

If it is assumed Johnson was hit on the head at that point, there is a strong likelihood that it was more than once. The lacerations showed that up to eight blows were struck. Since the injuries ran from the right forehead to the back of the skull, it is probable that Johnson, seated on the left behind the wheel, turned to the right to face the back seat when he was attacked. Mrs. Berard said Deacon was on the left side in the back seat when she got out and saw his left arm raised. Within the restricted confines of even a large automobile, it would be almost impossible for a man on the left side of the back seat to hit a man on the right side of the head wielding an eighteen-inch-long weapon in his left hand.

It is also questionable if what was indicated to be as many as eight blows could have been struck within the time frame indicated by Helen Berard's statements and in her demonstration given to Inspector Nicholson when she was taken in the cruiser to Kenaston Boulevard. Remember that her words were: "I grabbed the door handle to jump out when I saw Lorne raise his arm up. I was scared and I closed the door after me and turned and grabbed the handle. I noticed there was gravel under my feet and looked up in the cab and I didn't see the driver behind the wheel and I saw he was laying down on the seat... I am also sure it was his left arm that was raised as I was getting out of the cab." If that is the true story, Deacon would have had to have waited until she left the cab before moving to the right to strike a number of blows.

All this during the moment it took for her to slam the door and turn and look inside?

And, if it is assumed Deacon did accomplish that unlikely feat, then he would have had to get out of the taxi, open the door and push Johnson's body to the right, then climb behind the wheel. He would then have to have driven the cab half-a-mile south and turned left onto the track into the bush. There he would have gotten out, opened the right hand front door, grasped the body by the shoulders and pulled it from the car.

Spots that might have been blood on a handkerchief and an undershirt and nowhere else? No fingerprints in the car except those of the deceased?

Let us now turn to the murder weapon. Chief Justice Williams, in his charge to the jury, suggested that the murder weapon could readily have been carried by Deacon on the night of the slaying. With due respect to the late chief justice, that is a highly unlikely surmise. Recall that the paper-wrapped bolt was eighteen inches long, had a large square nut on one end and weighed close to three pounds. Deacon was a slight, slim man who dressed carefully. If the Crown's case is taken at face value, it would mean that Deacon prepared a weapon with string taken from his closet, then hid it somewhere in his fitted Chesterfield coat. It would have been visible in a pocket, and even if he put it up his sleeve it would reach from his wrist to his shoulder. He would surely not have been able to bend his arm. Would he then carry such a conspicuous encumbrance to an anniversary party with the aim of committing a robbery later?

That is obviously sheer nonsense. But, it was the prosecution's contention. Why else was the short piece of string found in the clothes closet brought to court as an exhibit, plus drawings and measurements of the closet where it was found? If that was not the Crown's theory, what other use did it have, other than to bolster a weak case? Discard that theory and speculate—unlikely as it is—that Deacon had the string in his pocket and fashioned the weapon when he was absent from the party for an interval, variously estimated at from 20 to 45 minutes. Where would he hide it on his return? None of the others at the party saw it. Helen Berard, in her various stories, first mentioned seeing a similar object on the back floor of the taxi when she claimed to have followed Deacon into the back seat. According to her story they had walked a considerable distance before hailing the cab. Surely it would have been visible during that time if he carried it into the cab with him? In retrospect, it must be concluded that Deacon did not have the murder weapon with him that evening, and did not take it into the taxi. If Johnson carried it in the taxi for his own defence because of the recent robberies of night-time drivers, why was it in the back seat? Strangely this is one of the few areas where Mrs. Berard changed her evidence-in-chief when cross-examined as a hostile witness by the Crown. She denied seeing the parcel and said she put it in her statement because Nicholson told her it was there. Recollect also that Deacon at one point tried to leave the party for a second time, and that Helen Berard and Allan Cooper went out and persuaded him to return.

Let us now turn to the mystery of why the taxicab should have drawn to a stop on the west side of Kenaston Boulevard about one-tenth of a mile south of Tuxedo Avenue on the road to nowhere in the middle of the night? The fact that there had been a recent series of taxi robberies made the question even more pertinent. Given the state of development in the area, it was the most unlikely of places for a taxi driver to have stopped if Helen Berard's statements to police, and her evidence at the inquest, were true. She said she asked the driver to stop when she and Deacon quarrelled en-route to Rosie's home in Charleswood; but it was impossible to get to Charleswood by travelling down Kenaston. Instead of proceeding down Kenaston past Tuxedo, the route would lead to the right on Tuxedo Avenue, then west on Roblin Road. It is true that, at the preliminary hearing, Mrs. Berard amended her earlier statements and placed the cab on

Roblin Road before it turned back. But that made the stop on Kenaston south of Tuxedo even more unlikely. That would have been away from the route back downtown. The only things lying to the south on Kenaston in 1946 were some very rough roads leading to very sparsely inhabited areas. The aerial photographs of the area in 1946 acquired by the author show not one dwelling south of Tuxedo Avenue on Kenaston Boulevard. At the south end, the road was in such abominable shape that Helen Berard's footprints were imprinted in the mud for days before they were found.

Maybe the mystery of the taxi's arrival at that deserted spot lay in the fact that, over the CNR tracks about a mile to the south, there was a rough trail leading to Parker Avenue? The affidavit filed in the appeal court by the two independent taxi drivers showed that, in her drunken middle of the night wanderings, Helen Berard was drawn to the Zrudlo home on Parker Avenue.

Whether deliberate or not, the police evidence downplayed the remoteness and sparse inhabitation of the murder scene. Searchers for clues in the area constantly referred to street names in their court evidence. Inspector Nicholson, for example, told of following a trail southeast from the clearing where the body was found to the intersection of two streets, which he named. Also, a map outlining the murder scene showed a grid of named streets taken from a plan of subdivision. The impression was thereby left in the minds of the jurors that it was at least a semi-developed area. That was far from the true condition at the time. The plan of subdivision was the remnant of a land bubble that had burst around 1914 when a British land development company went bankrupt. While the street pattern had been cleared of bush, it had long since deteriorated into a series of overgrown trails. My search for an aerial photo of the area was prompted by the memory of searching for wildflowers in the area in my youth. I recalled my astonishment at finding rusting fire hydrants and manhole covers—relics of that failed undertaking—deep in the bush during those rambles through the clearings and brush in search of Prairie Lilies.

Several other aspects of Helen Berard's statements deserve attention. Chief Justice Williams, in his summation, told the jury they could assume the taxi, taken by Deacon and Mrs. Berard, did not have a light on the top, leaving the clear inference that it had been the murdered man's cab. While it is true that she mentioned the light on top of the cab for the first time at the preliminary hearing, she continued to maintain that as fact throughout the trials.

Further, in the statement she gave Ayres shortly after she was taken to the police station, she gave the following description: "It was a navy blue cab and the meter was on the dash, and I didn't notice the name on it. The driver was a middle-aged fellow, not very big, and his hair was black, but he had a bald spot on the back of his head, and he wore a cap." While Johnson's cab was navy blue, the description of the driver does not fit, and the meter was not "on the dash," but was fitted onto a bracket. That evidence was constant throughout Helen Berard's testimony. She even furnished a drawing of the back of the driver's head to police.

The curious emphasis placed on the handkerchief embroidered with the initial "J" in one corner also bears examination. Mrs. Berard's stories were consistent throughout all her statements and sworn testimony that someone at the presumed scene of the murder had thrust something soft into her hand and told her to "take this and beat it," and that she had thrown it away after fleeing into the bush. She first attributed the statement to Deacon then to the mysterious man she said came on the scene in a second taxi. The question is, why would anyone who had just committed a violent crime bother to dispose of a clean, non-incriminating handkerchief? Yet, great emphasis was placed on that inconsequential act.

Adding to that mystery is the reference to a handkerchief in Helen Berard's statement written down by detectives immediately after she was taken to the police station. In an odd sentence, completely out of context and bearing no apparent relationship to what she was talking about, she said: "A week before that Saturday I was with my girl friend, Jean Gauthier, Lorette, Man., and we were downtown, and I had forgotten my hanky, and she gave me an Irish linen hanky with a 'J' in the corner."

That opens a new line of speculation that Mrs. Berard was being closely questioned on specifics by detectives, and her statement was not spontaneous and uninterrupted as alleged in evidence to the courts, but a series of answers written down in continuity. Either Ayres asked her about the handkerchief that had been found on Kenaston, or she was trying to cover up something else. She had no reason to extricate herself, having already placed herself in a taxi on Kenaston. A "J" could as easily signify Jean Gauthier, Johann Johnson, or Joe Zrudlo.

Only one thing is certain in this tangled web of uncertainties. The Hon. E.J. McMurray voiced it in his final summation to the second jury. Helen Berard was "a liar and a prodigious one." Mr. Justice A.K. Dysart expounded it a little less directly in writing his separate judgement on the second appeal when he noted that the conviction rested mainly on the evidence of Mrs. Berard. He added: "In arriving at their verdict, the jury must have rejected the exculpatory parts of Berard's testimony in chief, and substituted therefore the prior inconsistent statements. To find where the truth lay in those conflicting statements—if it existed in any of them—the jury needed the soundest possible guidance of the trial judge." In a later reference he said that Mrs. Berard "must have perjured herself either in her prior inquest testimony or in her trial evidence—or perhaps in both."

That latter observation deserves study. Was it a simple case of either/or? Counting the garbled version she gave to the two taxi drivers while out on bail, she related four distinct stories. In the first of the written statements presented to the courts, she fled the scene leaving Deacon alone in the taxi with the driver. In the next, she implicated him directly by saying she saw his left arm raised and the driver slumped on the front seat. The third version, related at the preliminary hearing and maintained at both trials, saw the cab bearing Deacon drive away and another taxi appear on the scene. In the tearful, self-pitying ramblings to the two taxi drivers, Deacon was not in the taxi. She flagged down a taxi and a stranger was already in it.

Which is most plausible? The latter story is the least worthy of consideration. A man bent on committing a crime would not invite a witness to attend. Both juries chose the second story that Deacon was the man with the upraised arm. Both trial judges appeared to agree. Chief Justice Williams told the jury that the part of the story about a second car appearing was "incredible."

But, was it? After reading and rereading the evidence, and considering the point at which the death car came to a stop on Kenaston, I would accept that a second car might well have arrived. It is beyond comprehension that an experienced cab driver would divert from a direct route to turn right and drive down a deserted, unlit road in the middle of the night to let a drunken woman out. He would have stopped under the lights on Tuxedo Avenue, or have turned left onto the northern, inhabited part of Kenaston where there were also street lights. Only a driver under threat from a weapon might be forced to drive south of Tuxedo on Kenaston and stop.

Consider now another possibility that falls somewhere between the second car version and the story told to the taxi drivers of getting into a taxi with a strange man. Helen Berard appeared to have no qualms about contacting male drinking companions in the middle of the night. Is it possible that she left 1064 Dudley and walked alone to Corydon and Stafford where she got into a taxi that came along, but that the man inside was no stranger? Could she have phoned and asked somebody to come and pick her up at that point?

Whatever the truth might have been, Helen Berard was to

have another opportunity to testify to what really happened.

On Friday, April 9, Justice Minister J.L. Ilsley issued a terse statement in Ottawa. The federal cabinet, after careful consideration, was unable to advise the governor-general to interfere with the sentence of the court. The following Monday, an eight-column headline on the front page of the *Winnipeg Free Press* dramatically proclaimed: "Star Witness Flies To Save Deacon; Mrs. Berard Races To Ottawa." The front page of the *Winnipeg Tribune* was no less sensational: "Mrs. Berard Pleading For The Life Of Deacon; Waits To See Ilsley To Bid Against Death." The drama was to dominate the front pages for the rest of the week. Leaving Calgary aboard a Trans-Canada Airlines plane Monday morning, Mrs. Berard talked briefly with Harry Walsh during a short stop in Winnipeg before continuing to Ottawa. She avoided the press, but was quoted as saying she was now ready to "tell the real story."

When she arrived in Ottawa before noon that same day, Helen Berard appeared near collapse. Newsmen reported that she seemed scarcely able to speak, and her lips quivered as she answered one or two questions in monosyllables. She was met by her mother, Mrs. D. Cameron of Dumbarton, Ontario, a short, hostile woman with braided grey hair, who effectively kept reporters at bay. Brusquely shielding her daughter from questions, she whisked her to their motel room and refused to answer the door or the phone.

The elderly woman was equally effective the next day in fending off the press when she and her daughter arrived at the Justice Building for a private interview with Ilsley. Leaving the minister's office some 40 minutes later, Mrs. Berard and her mother walked at a fast clip through the group of reporters in the hall with Ilsley walking behind them. The two women dashed through a door leading to an interior stairway while the justice minister stopped at the door to fend off questions. Helen Berard looked downcast and pale as she and her mother ran up to the next floor and escaped through a back exit to avoid photographers waiting at the front door. It was the last glimpse the Ottawa newsmen would get of the mother and daughter. What Helen Berard told the justice minister was to remain a secret. Their motel reported that they had checked out, and they were not to be found at any other hotel in Ottawa, nor at Dumbarton.

Ilsley would only say he would report what Mrs. Berard had told him to cabinet. Any decision on the matter would be announced by the secretary of state. The justice minister, who had spent the weekend reading through the evidence given at the trials, reported to Prime Minister King and his cabinet on Wednesday. The next morning a final communique was issued by E.H. Coleman, under-secretary of state. It read: "His excellency the Governor-General-in-Council is unable to order interference with the sentence of the court in the case of Lawrence Deacon, now under sentence of death."

In Dumbarton 25 miles outside Toronto, a local reporter finally caught up with Helen Berard at her parents' home. Again, Mrs. Cameron shielded her daughter and answered all the questions. "We only told Mr. Ilsley the same story over again. There was nothing new to tell. We told no-one anything new," said Mrs. Cameron. Unfortunately, the reporter did not ask which of her stories Helen Berard had told again, and the archival files in Ottawa, at least those to which I had access, offer no clue as to what she told the justice minister.

At Headingley jail all was in readiness for the execution, now only a few short hours away. Hangman Camille Branchaud had already stretched the rope with a sack of sand approximately Deacon's weight, and was standing by. Shortly before noon on Thursday, April 15, Sheriff D.C.M. Kyle visited Deacon and told him that Ottawa had refused to commute his sentence. It was only then that Deacon learned of Mrs. Berard's frantic flight to Ottawa. Laying aside the book he was reading—*Tomorrow is Forever* by Gwen Bristow—Deacon took the news calmly.

His former employer, H.J. Gray, dogged to the last, sent off a final telegram to Justice Minister Ilsley that afternoon: "I, H.J. Gray, Canadian-born subject, veteran of the First World War and former employer of Lawrence Deacon, do most humbly beseech and request clemency; so that I may retain faith in Canadian justice." Then he and his wife went to break the news to Deacon's mother. She had continued to the last to walk from door to door on Toronto and Victor Streets getting signatures on the petitions still going forward to Ottawa. Facing the finality of the decision without tears, Beatrice Deacon could only keep repeating: "If he's got to go, he's got to go." That afternoon she visited her son for the last time.

On that final afternoon, Harry Walsh also visited Deacon in his cell where he was given the doomed man's written statement maintaining his innocence and thanking those who had worked on his behalf. Then Walsh walked down 13 steps to the second condemned cell located directly below the one leading into the execution chamber. There Michael Angelo Vescio looked up from the western novels that were his only diversion. Speaking through the small square of bars on the cell door, Walsh told Vescio that the Manitoba Court of Appeal had that morning dismissed his appeal by a three to two margin.

Shortly before midnight, I approached the brightly lit front of Headingley Jail and presented my pass at the door. Extra precautions had been taken following rumours that a protest demonstration was to take place outside the jail. Floodlights lit up the front yard, and additional RCMP officers had been assigned to patrol the approaches to the jail. But, the drive to save Deacon had apparently exhausted itself in the last bitter moments, and the demonstration failed to develop.

In the waiting room beside the warden's office, the *Winnipeg Tribune* reporter and I managed to swallow a few gulps of scotch from my flask, but it did little to relieve the tension. Shortly before 1 a.m. a guard motioned to us and the other witnesses to follow him. As he unlocked the barred iron doors leading toward the execution chamber, the rasp of the key in the huge lock, and the clang of the doors closing behind us, assaulted an unreal silence. There was not a sound from the line of cells flanking the corridor leading to the final steel door. But you knew that, inside those cells, not a single man was asleep. It was a silence you could hear, as though everyone had simultaneously drawn their breath and sucked away all the air, leaving a vacuum within the jail.

Numb with apprehension of what was to come, I stood with the others in a silent semicircle behind the railing separating us from the gallows. At 1:05 a.m. the door on the east wall swung open. A voice said, "Let him walk alone." Flanked by two guards, his face ashen but composed, Deacon walked in followed by his chaplain and the hangman. Moments before, the hangman had entered the condemned cell by the other door and pinioned the condemned man's arms behind his back, but not before Deacon shook hands with his guards and thanked them for their treatment of him.

Glancing quickly around, Deacon walked steadily to the scaffold and stood there erect. As the hangman placed a hood over his head and adjusted the noose, Deacon repeated the Lord's Prayer in a calm voice in response to Reverend Anderson. Moving swiftly in what seemed a single motion, the hangman bent and strapped Deacon's legs together then reached for the heavy lever. Reverend Anderson was beginning a second prayer when the heavy doors dropped open with a reverberating bang. Less than a minute had passed since Deacon had entered the chamber. It was not yet 1:06 a.m. A man who had his neck wounded overseas in the service of his country, had just had it broken in the name of justice.

On the other side of the east wall of the pit below the gallows, where Deacon's body hung suspended, Vescio lay on his cot. In the unlikely event that he had been asleep, the thunderous bang of the trapdoors echoing through the jail would surely have wakened him. Tomorrow he would move upstairs where the door on the west wall of the cell opened to eternity.

At 1:19 a.m., Dr. E.K. Vann, the prison doctor, nodded his head. Deacon's body was lowered from the scaffold and a coroner's inquest convened before a jury of seven of the local residents of the Headingley area. Shortly afterwards the body was taken through a door in the south wall of the pit. In a flower-draped casket, it was lifted into a waiting hearse and taken to Mordue's funeral home. At 7:30 a.m. on that cool April morning a simple ceremony took place in St. James Cemetery as Lawrence Deacon was buried. His mother, Mr. and Mrs. Gray, Col. Churchill and members of the Deacon Defence Fund stood with heads bowed as the coffin was lowered into the ground.

They were convinced that an innocent man had been hanged, and, in the minds of thousands of Winnipeg residents, there was more than a reasonable doubt of his guilt. Only Helen Elizabeth Berard knew the answer.

Chapter Six

Cold Blooded Murder

The Vescio case is one that most Winnipeggers over 50 years of age appear to remember most vividly. It also appears to be one that geography and archival records want to forget; almost as though to deny that the terror that stalked the streets for over a year ever existed.

Few people in today's rush hour traffic that sweeps over the Mid-Town Bridge crossing the Assiniboine River near the city centre, realize that they are passing the scene where the horror began. Before the Mid-Town Bridge eased the traffic congestion to and from the heart of the city, a quiet little backwater of modest working class homes mingled with small industrial establishments on the south side of the river where the extension of downtown Donald Street now swings traffic to Osborne Street and on to the suburbs to the south. In early January 1946, Moore's Coal and Wood Yard lay hard alongside the CNR railway tracks where Stradbrook Avenue bisects the new extension of Donald. Across what was then Clarke Street, stood a small two-storey home where 13-year-old Roy Ewan McGregor lived with his parents, his sister Adele, 15, his uncle Jim Ewan and a cousin, Alice Morden.

Today an 18-storey apartment block stands where the coal and wood yard used to be, and the extension of Donald Street has long since obliterated that section of Clarke Street where the McGregor home stood. A short distance away, between what remains of Clarke Street and Osborne Street, Rose Street ran one block to a dead end off River Avenue. A researcher, seeking to reconstruct the crime today, would have a hard time. Not only has all but one block of Clarke Street disappeared, but Rose Street, where Michael Angelo Vescio was billeted by the army, has been renamed Bole Street.

And, if the researcher began his quest in the Manitoba Archives Building, he would find that the Court of King's Bench pocket, containing details of Vescio's trial, had disappeared. At the Manitoba Archives warehouse in west Winnipeg, where the Manitoba Court of Appeal records are kept, he would face similar frustration. The Vescio records cannot be found. Should he persist in the search and seek out the library files of the defunct *Winnipeg Tribune*, housed at the University of Manitoba, he would draw another blank. The Vescio files disappeared before the U of M archives received the *Tribune* records. Fortunately, the file in the *Winnipeg Free Press* library was committed to microfilm and still exists. However, that library is no longer open to the public, other than by special arrangement.

The best way to reconstruct the events then, is to patiently screen back through the microfilm copies of the daily newspapers of the period. In January 1946, the typographers at the Winnipeg newspapers were on strike and a combined issue was being produced under the double banner of the *Winnipeg Free Press* and *Winnipeg Tribune*. There the story begins on the front page of the combined issue of Saturday, January 5, 1946:

"The bullet-pierced body of 13-year-old Roy Ewan McGregor, of 149 Clarke St., was found at 8:30 a.m. today by Fort Rouge police huddled in a coal bin in Moore's Coal and Wood Yard, 158 Clarke St., just opposite the boy's home.

"The boy had been shot in the pit of the stomach and through the forehead by what police believe was a 38 calibre revolver.

"Death was instantaneous police say.

"No trace of the weapon has been found.

"'It looks like cold-blooded murder,' stated Deputy Chief

Charles MacIver, who investigated the case along with city detectives this morning."

That same morning Private Michael Vescio, a driver in the Royal Canadian Army Service Corps, was leaning against the back of the motor pool garage at Fort Osborne Barracks smoking a cigarette. One of the other drivers turned from where he was reading that same front page: "Say Vescio that happened in your district didn't it?" Vescio replied calmly: "Yeah, and I think I might have seen that fellow."

The previous evening, young McGregor and Victor Flower, son of a Fort Rouge policeman, had gone to a movie. Returning from downtown, they stopped for a milk shake at the Dutch Maid Ice Cream Parlour on Osborne Street where the boutiques and restaurants of Osborne Village now line both sides of the street. Afterwards they walked south to the intersection of Gertrude Avenue where they parted about 11:10 p.m. Roy crossed the street, where he talked with two other young friends for about five minutes at the streetcar stop. He then walked east on Gertrude Avenue toward his home. That was the last time he was seen alive.

About 11:45 p.m. Snowball, a small Pomeranian dog, began to bark and run up and down the yard at 248 Stradbrook Avenue, just north of Moore's coal yard. His antics had been triggered by the sound of a shot, followed several minutes later by another. Unaware of the shots, but aroused by the barking, Snowball's owner, Mrs. J. Puchniak, went to her kitchen window. Thinking that someone might be trying to steal her hens, she stood at the window for some 20 minutes, but could see nothing.

In the McGregor home, Roy's mother was becoming concerned at his failure to return home. After phoning the Flower's home and learning that Roy had headed toward home around 11:10 a.m., she and her husband Allistair, aided by her brother Jim Ewan, began a search of the district. Finding no trace, they phoned the police at 2 a.m. and then maintained the search until 3:30 a.m. At 8:15 a.m. Roman Klibak, the yardman, turned on the light in the coal bin at the yard and found the body.

Some 66 yards from the coal bin, police found a pool of blood in the snow near an empty boxcar drawn up on a spur leading from the CNR tracks into the coal yard. Roy McGregor had obviously been shot at that point and his body was then dragged to the coal bin. Over that weekend every available detective was on duty, and a search began that was to make history in the field of criminal investigation.

By the middle of the following week, it had become evident that Roy McGregor had been sexually assaulted before he was shot. Similar assaults that had taken place within four blocks of each other over the previous four months were reported to police. In one of them, the boy was shown a gun and told; "Shut up, or I will shoot."

The current euphemism "gay" to denote homosexual behaviour had not yet been coined. Rather, the police and the newspapers passed judgement in harsh terms on any perceived or imagined homosexual tendencies. Thus, the combined *Winnipeg Free Press* and *Winnipeg Tribune* of Thursday, January 10, proclaimed:

"Criminal haunts throughout the city are being combed clean, and all known sex perverts are being brought to police headquarters for grilling, in the all-out manhunt for the slayer of Roy McGregor.

"Police are being flooded with calls reporting suspicious acts. Inspector of Detectives William McPherson stated today that 'a few years ago our file of known sex perverts in the city totalled 250 or 300 at most. Now the city seems to be flooded with them.'

"This pointed up the theory held by police that the sadistic slayer of young McGregor is a sex pervert."

Over the following weeks police visited Winnipeg schools, particularly in the Fort Rouge area, warning boys gathered in the school auditoriums to beware of a man whose practice was to stop boys, ask them about a certain address, then to accompany him to point out the location. At the same time, they asked any boy who might have been accosted to report to them.

Gradually, the early panic subsided. But, from time to time, police issued warnings that a dangerous criminal was still at large and precautions should continue to be taken.

No new facts emerged at the inquest into the death of Roy McGregor and newsmen speculated that, if the police had any clues that might lead to the apprehension of the killer, they were not revealing them. That theory was more nearly correct than they realized. Winnipeg police were in possession of a clue that would lead Michael Vescio to the gallows; but they were playing their cards very carefully and revealing nothing. In fact, they were putting out misleading signals to throw the murderer off guard.

At 9 p.m. on the day Roy McGregor's body was found, a clerk at Moore's coal and wood yard had pointed out a spent nine-millimetre shell casing to Detective Robert Young. It was lying three feet from the vacant railway boxcar near where the pool of blood had been found in the yard. When Young picked it up, he noted there was ice on the snow beneath it, showing that the shell casing was warm when it fell. Shortly afterwards, another shell casing and a live cartridge were found nearby.

A hasty conference was held that afternoon in the detective offices and a mine detector was borrowed from the army. After cordoning off the coal yard from prying eyes, the police began a painstaking search with the mine detector. Since the area was littered with nails, bottle caps and scrap metal, they buried a nail, a bottle top and a copper-jacketed bullet and tested each separately. They found that the bullet gave off a different sound and the officers, who operated the detector in 20-minute shifts, were taught to identify the variety of pings emanating from the earphones.

On the third day a bullet was found imbedded about four inches in the ground under snow and ice. It, along with the shell casings, was sent to the RCMP Crime Detection Laboratory in

Regina. There, ballistics expert Sgt. A. Mason Rooke began a lengthy process of elimination by comparing the width of striations made by the barrel rifling, and imprints left on the spent shell casing by the firing pin and extractor. Although there were at least ten different types of nine-millimetre pistols manufactured, Rooke could report by the end of February that he had ruled out all types with exception of the nine-millimetre Browning automatic manufactured by John Inglis Company of Toronto for the Canadian army. Confidential letters immediately went out to all police forces in North America describing the weapon and asking them to report if a similar pistol turned up.

In Winnipeg, police issued a routine bulletin asking returned servicemen to register any handguns they might have retained as war souvenirs. When I responded by taking in a nine-millimetre Luger I had acquired on Liberation Day in Copenhagen, they simply gave it a cursory glance and handed it back with a registration slip. However, any Brownings were test fired and the bullets sent to Regina for examination. But, the trail remained cold.

Then, on Thursday, September 19, nine months after the McGregor murder, the body of 13-year-old George Robert Smith was found sprawled face down in a muddy lane between Home and Arlington Streets in Winnipeg's west end. The body was stripped to the waist, and a bullet had been fired into the back just below the right shoulder blade.

Young George had last been seen about 10 p.m. the night before, when he and three other boys left a scout meeting at Home Street United Church near Portage Avenue. They walked a block north on Home Street to St. Matthews Avenue. As they stood there talking, a woman came out of a nearby house and told them they should be home in bed. The boys parted and George walked alone toward his home a block-and-a-half further north at 585 Home Street.

When he did not arrive home by 11 p.m., his father phoned

police to ask if any accidents had been reported. He then began an all-night search for his son. At 1 a.m. George's aunt, Helen MacGregor, who lived with the Smiths, phoned police and reported him missing. At 7:15 a.m. a neighbour across the street from the Smith home backed his car out of his garage. Checking over his shoulder to see if the lane was clear, he was startled to see a body in the lane. Running back into the house, he asked his wife to call police.

Detective James Mulholland began searching the area after arriving at the scene of the second slaying about 8 a.m. Shortly afterwards he noticed a jagged crease on a slat of a low fence surrounding a garden behind 591 Arlington Street next door to a house under construction. Reasoning that it might have been made by a bullet, Mulholland lined up the crease with the garden and calculated that the bullet might be found in a three foot square area of the garden.

Again the mine detector was brought into action. Late that afternoon, the copper-jacketed bullet that had passed through George Smith's body and snuffed out his life was found about two inches under the earth in the garden. Meanwhile, Mulholland's partner, Albert Manning, had found an empty nine-millimetre shell casing nearby. The bullet and casing were dispatched to Regina. Sgt. Rooke wired back the results of the ballistics test. Both boys had been killed by the same gun. Again, the police were cautious. No mention of their find was made at the inquest into young Smith's death. They now knew they were after a serial killer who had kept the gun after the first slaying. If they revealed that it could be identified, he might dispose of the evidence.

Without knowledge of that absolute evidence, Winnipeggers reached the same conclusion; that a serial killer was loose in their midst. New panic gripped the city as every available man on the Winnipeg police force was thrown into an around-the-clock search for the killer.

Tips and leads flooded into the switchboard at the central

police station, and special squads were detailed to investigate each call. To make up for a shortage of cruiser cars, "U" drives were hired and cars on loan from concerned citizens were pressed into use. Daily newspapers carried appeals for aid from the public. A two-column box on the front page of the *Free Press* appealed to readers to "Help Catch A Killer," and urged parents to question their children about any suspicious men who might approach them and to warn them not to enter a lane, building, or any other secluded place with a stranger.

One man was foolish enough to approach a young boy on Good Street, and after informing him that he was a policeman, asked the youngster to go with him. The boy let out a yell, and a recently discharged army veteran raced across the street to his aid. When police arrived, the impostor was stretched out cold. He had been felled by a hard right hook.

Within a week of the second slaying, rewards totalling $7,000 had been offered for information leading to apprehension of the killer. Boy scouts going to and from weekly meetings were urged to travel in groups. The school board ruled that children aged 13 and under would not be allowed to attend the popular high school football games unless accompanied by a parent or older student. While some trustees wanted the games cancelled altogether, a compromise was made by starting the football games early and moving as many as possible to Saturday mornings.

Despite the intensity of the manhunt, few tangible new clues emerged and the fear remained. Throughout the winter, police constantly reminded parents that the murderer was still at large and urged them to accompany their children to meetings after dark, or have them travel in groups.

On January 14, 1947, just over one year after the death of Roy McGregor, Chief Constable George Smith retired. His last message was a final warning to parents to stay vigilant. Expressing regret that he had to retire before the murderer was caught, Chief Smith declared: "These are the most vicious murders we've ever heard of. They are unparalleled in the continent's crime records. There are no records of any killings more vicious."

As winter gave way to spring the vigil relaxed somewhat, and as the summer passed with no similar violent incidents, reminders of the killings faded from the pages of the Winnipeg newspapers. Then, on Tuesday, July 29, I was handed a story that young cub reporters can only dream about.

It had been a quiet morning on the law courts beat. Just before noon the *Tribune* reporter, Bruce Larson, and I left the second floor press room in the Manitoba Law Courts Building on Broadway to walk back to our offices. We were about to walk down the stairs when one of the sheriff's officers approached and said someone wanted to see me for a moment in his office. Telling Larson to wait a minute and that I would be right back, I left him talking to the sheriff's man. Fortunately, Larson was only standing in for the regular *Tribune* law courts reporter who was away. Otherwise, I might not have gotten away with what followed.

What I learned in that short minute from an absolutely reliable source in an office off the main corridor was that the gun used to kill the two boys was in Regina and had been positively identified. My source added that it had been taken from a man arrested following a holdup in Port Arthur, Ontario (since amalgamated with Fort William to become Thunder Bay) and that the man was in Stony Mountain penitentiary serving a three-year sentence.

With the biggest story that could possibly break in Winnipeg in my grasp, I walked as calmly as I could back to where Larson was waiting.

"What did he want you for?"

"Oh nothing. He just wanted to thank me for a small favour I did for him."

Basically that answer was the truth. My informant had given me the tip as thanks for a favour I had done for him a short time earlier, and because he had learned that I would keep my source of information confidential.

That half-mile walk to Graham Avenue and Carlton Street, where Larson and I parted, was agony. When he crossed Carlton and continued toward the *Tribune* building some three blocks away, I broke into a run down Carlton Street. Without waiting for the elevator in the *Free Press* building, I went up the stairs to the fourth floor city room two steps at a time. Panting from the exertion, I blurted what I knew in the ear of Eddie Armstong, our city editor.

Eddie gave me a startled look, then jumped up and dragged me by the arm into the small editor's office behind the city desk and closed the door. A former sports editor, Eddie had contacts with almost everyone in Winnipeg. Within minutes he was on the telephone to Chief Constable Charles MacIver. When Eddie told him what we knew, MacIver was startled.

"You can't print that story."

"Why not? We know it's true Charlie, and we're getting close to deadline."

"Yes it's true, but you can't print it. Don't say anything to anyone; I'll be right there."

Putting down the receiver, Eddie told me that something was up and we should go back to the city room and not say anything. Five minutes later, I saw Chief MacIver walk across the city room and disappear into the back office with Eddie.

Shortly afterwards the chief came out. As he disappeared into the elevator, Eddie beckoned me back to the editor's office. After the door was closed, I learned what the chief had said. "We're holding off. He says it's absolutely true, but the man has given them an alibi. Says he got the gun from a sergeant-major in the army after the murders took place. The chief says they don't believe him, but they can't take any chances. He says that if the alibi really is true and we run the story, then the guilty man may cover up. He wants time to complete the investigation. Says that, if we hold off, he will give us a straight 24-hour scoop on everybody else when the murder charges are laid."

If I thought the walk back to the office had been nerve-wracking, the next ten days were going to be excruciating. Over the next week we put the whole story together by checking back on Canadian Press stories from Port Arthur, and two others were drawn in and sworn to secrecy. The news editor, Orton Grain, wrote the story and a typographer set the lead type one evening. Wrapped in newspaper, it was hidden at the back of the editor's office awaiting the signal from Chief MacIver.

Over the rest of the week that signal never came. Each day, after the copies of the *Tribune* had been picked up and distributed around our office, we grabbed them and scanned the front page with dread; then heaved a sigh of relief that the secret was still ours.

I was at home when the telephone rang just after dinner on Thursday, August 7. It was my informant. He had news. Winnipeg police were going to bring Vescio in from the penitentiary the next morning and charge him with the murders of the boys. We still hadn't heard from Chief MacIver that the investigation was finished. I telephoned Eddie. It was time for a strategy session.

The next morning Gordon Sinclair (no relation to the late Gordon Sinclair of Toronto) who covered the city police beat, was brought into the picture. He was to watch the detective office at the Rupert Avenue police station and report back when he saw the suspect brought in. At 11:30 a.m. he reported that detectives had driven into the police garage and had taken a man up the back stairs to the detective office. He thought it was our man Vescio. Eddie still hadn't heard from the chief.

That afternoon the presses started at the 2 p.m. deadline as usual. The main front page story bore a deep eight-column headline: "Churchill Flays Socialists." Under that head was a British United Press story and a picture of Winston Churchill. It was a decoy. Downstairs I was waiting at the back door of the circulation department. When the *Tribune* driver picked up their usual copies of the *Free Press* as as it came hot off the presses and departed, I telephoned upstairs.

The *Tribune* truck had barely rounded the corner when the presses in the basement of the *Free Press* building ground to a halt. Only 400 of the "Churchill" issue had been run off, and they were being dumped. Downstairs went the newspaper wrapped lead type from the editor's office. The front page was unlocked, the decoy story removed and the murder story locked in its place. Then the presses started again. The story announcing the break in the McGregor and Smith cases was on the street for an hour before the *Tribune* police reporter bought a copy on his way back to his office from the police station.

We still hadn't heard from the chief, but we had our scoop and it was too late for the opposition to replate. Their press run was over for the day. They would have to catch up the next day.

Eddie Armstrong's wife and family were away, so the victory party moved to his suburban Norwood home that night. The celebration was well under way when Eddie's telephone rang. It was Chief MacIver. He was belatedly keeping his pledge on our 24-hour exclusive, but he was not happy about it. Barricaded in his Niagara Street home in River Heights, he had taken the telephone off the hook and was refusing to answer the door to the persistent reporters from the *Tribune* and the radio stations who were camped outside. Eddie came back grinning: "He wants to know where we got the story. I wouldn't even give him a hint. He's really steaming." We raised a collective toast to the chief and continued the party.

The telephone jangled again. This time it was Mayor Garnet Coulter who was also chairman of the Winnipeg Police Commission. He called to congratulate Eddie and the *Free Press* for withholding the story until the police investigation was complete. While expressing his thanks, he added: "And, of course, you know the man has confessed." We didn't know, but Eddie replied; "Yes, of course."

We had scarcely finished hoisting a toast to the mayor when the telephone rang again. Increasingly frustrated at his enforced confinement, it was Chief MacIver again. He was still trying to find out where we got our tips. He received no more satisfaction than the first time. In fact, he nearly came through the telephone when Eddie casually remarked that we knew Vescio had confessed. Eddie wasn't ready to reveal that he had just learned it from the mayor when the chief bellowed: "How the hell did you find that out?"

Ignoring the need for judicial process, we tried, convicted and executed Vescio in that first story. Using the colourful rhetoric of the period, the first paragraph proclaimed: "The long, red trail of bestial death and terror today appeared pointed directly at the gallows."

If that was trial by front page, worse was yet to come. The chief joined in the next morning by issuing a lengthy statement at a press conference in his office. Topping a front page completely devoted to the murder charges against Vescio was the headline: "Killings Confessed Chief Announces." In addition, the staffs of both daily papers had been turned loose to dig up every conceivable angle on the story. There was column after column and page after page of copy. There were interviews with Vescio's landlord on Rose Street, the Port Arthur police, soldiers who had served with Vescio and anyone else who had contact with him in any way. There were pictures of the dead boys, of their homes and of the police using the mine detector to find the bullets.

The following Monday further stories dominated the front pages. Disdaining the fact that the criminal record of an accused person cannot be revealed because it could influence potential jurors, one story was headed: "Vescio Termed Ringleader In Lakehead Armed Holdup." There was not a faint hope of finding a juror in Winnipeg, or Manitoba, who could say he or she was unprejudiced. Looking back, it is hard to believe that contempt of court charges were not laid against both Winnipeg newspapers.

Even Vescio's brother, sister and his 64-year-old father in Port Arthur were interviewed. Informed by telephone that his son had been charged with murder, the stricken father blurted: "Kill, kill? Mike kill. I no believe. There is something wrong someplace. Mike he is in army all time. How he kill? Somebody who see will prove he no kill." However, the newspapers had left no doubts in anyone else's mind. Even before the evidence was presented at the preliminary hearings on the two murder charges, the newspaper readers knew the story in infinite detail. Vescio's life, from the cradle to his impending grave, had been laid open to the public.

Disregarding the sometimes visceral condemnation that permeated the general reporting, the picture that emerged was of a painfully shy, immature young man with a juvenile imagination. Michael Angelo Vescio stole a gun and his imagination led him out of his lonely ineptitude into the unreality of being a tough guy.

His father emigrated to Canada from Italy in 1902 and settled in Port Arthur. One of eight children, Michael led a withdrawn childhood concentrated almost solely within the family. His mother lavished special attention on the quiet child and was always there to salve his bumps and bruises. Growing up in a devout Roman Catholic household, he became an altar boy at St. Anthony church, but because of his shyness found school a necessary evil. Nervous and quiet, he did not talk very much and made few firm friends. When he was 14, his beloved mother died. Four years later, when he reached the minimum enlistment age of 18, "Mickey," as he was known to his family, enlisted in the Canadian army.

If the shy, withdrawn young man expected that enlistment in the armed services during wartime would bring excitement to his life, it was not to be. He was posted to Winnipeg with the Royal Canadian Army Service Corps, and there he remained for the duration of the war driving army vehicles on routine jobs. Not only was the expected excitement of overseas service denied him, the rough camaraderie of barracks life that might have shaken the young, withdrawn boy out of his shyness, was denied him as well. He was billeted out in a small room miles from the barracks and began a drab routine of commuting back and forth each day.

Now separated from his family 500 miles away in Port Arthur, and unable to cultivate close relationships because of his innate shyness, Vescio sank into a lonely humdrum routine. At the army motor pool the older men were quick to note that their slight, youthful companion was apparently not interested in girls. This although his olive complexion, dark eyes and neatly groomed dark hair would have made him attractive to many of them. His landlady at 115 Rose Street said that, although he was small and slight at five-feet-five-inches, "he was a very handsome fellow." Her husband, Sidney Wright, attributed his lack of interest in the opposite sex to his shy nature: "He would sooner run a mile than face a girl." His army companions were less understanding. With the reverse logic that dominated service relationships and earned a bald man the nickname "curly," they dubbed Vescio "killer." Ironically, the nickname stuck for the rest of his army career.

Over the three years that Vescio was billeted in the small second-floor room on Rose Street, he came to call Mr. and Mrs. Wright "mum" and "dad." Each morning he rose early and left for the barracks about 7 a.m. At 5:30 each evening he returned to the tiny, neatly kept room, and cleaned up before stopping in the downstairs living room to say hello to "mum." The dull pattern was unvarying. From there, a two-block walk brought him to Osborne Street and supper at the Margaret Rose Tea-Room.

Supper was followed on most evenings by a visit to the bookstore next door to the tea-room to pick up some light reading, magazines or comic books, and to buy cigarettes. From there it was back to his room to spend the rest of the evening lying on his bed reading and smoking. The door was always left open, and sometimes other soldiers billeted in the house dropped in to talk. Vescio would chat with them, but never went out of his way to make friends. He told an approving "mum" that, "the boys want me to go to the beer parlour with them and get tight, but I don't want to do that." If he wasn't reading, he would go for long walks alone.

Part of the unbroken routine was a visit each Saturday morning to the Fort Rouge Hairdressers on Osborne Street. There, barber Mel Bruce gave him a haircut, a shave and slicked his hair with tonic. Sunday was given over to a visit to Brookings Drug Store on Osborne for magazines and the rest of the day was spent in reading. Away from his father's strict Catholic influence, the former altar boy never once went to church in Winnipeg. Without fail, every Monday night saw Michael Vescio leave the house alone, saying he was going to a movie.

When detectives, making a routine search of the area in January 1946, following the shocking death of young Roy McGregor, visited 115 Rose Street and asked the Wrights about anyone in the area answering the description of a suspect, the landlady gave no thought to her gentlemanly young roomer. And there was no suspicion in the mind of her husband, although Vescio had brought down a pistol to show them around New Year's, within days of the McGregor murder. "We never thought anything of it. If a soldier didn't have a gun, who would?"

But, there was no reason Private Vescio, an RCASC driver serving in Canada, should have been issued a sidearm. The Browning had been issued to a sergeant-major in the Provost Corps at Fort Osborne Barracks. Vescio stole it one day when he was detailed to transport a work party out to Grassmere drainage ditch on the outskirts of Winnipeg. By a quirk of fate, an error in recording meant the gun was improperly listed and army officials were balked in their efforts to trace the missing weapon.

Strangely, Vescio's army associates never questioned the fact that he had a service issue sidearm. With a typical show of bravado that masked his inner uncertainties, Vescio showed the weapon to other drivers. On one occasion, when on convoy duty to the Shilo army camp in western Manitoba, Vescio pulled the Browning from inside his battle-dress jacket and fired several shots at some deer. He missed. And, he openly approached a sergeant-major in the stores to scrounge nine-millimetre ammunition, which was given to him on several occasions.

Vescio's army career ended with his discharge at Fort Osborne Barracks in February 1947. Despite entreaties from his father, who had remarried in 1946, to return home to Port Arthur, he stayed on in the room at Rose Street living on his army severance pay. "Why should I go back there? There's no job for me," he told the Wrights.

The older Vescio's persistence paid off in May when he wrote that there was a job waiting for Michael in Port Arthur. Vescio returned to his father's and stepmother's home at 334 Dufferin Street in Port Arthur, taking the stolen Browning with him. There he could not resist showing it off to his family, telling them that an officer in Winnipeg had given it to him. The officer, he said, told him to keep it quiet or it would be taken away from him.

Just over a month after he had returned home, Vescio and an 18-year-old companion, Frank George Guarasel, walked into the Port Arthur offices of Palm Dairies Limited on the afternoon of June 30. Both were wearing masks and brandishing guns. Foreman Sidney Patchett, with Robert Jones and John Morehead, was checking over the cash from the day's business. Herding the trio into a corner at gun-point, Vescio ordered them to face the wall. He then reached over and cut the telephone connection while Guarasel scooped up $380 from the till.

Tough guy Vescio was living out a real life fantasy. When Patchett said he did not know where the keys to a car parked in the yard were, Vescio cocked the Browning and waved it threateningly under his nose. Patchett surrendered the keys and Vescio stood guard while his young accomplice ran outside to start the car. Shortly afterward, the car horn sounded and Vescio dashed from the building.

Unable to use the telephone, one of the dairy employees ran to a nearby store and telephoned the police. Port Arthur police found the stolen car abandoned a short time later and a watch was established on all routes leading out of the twin Lakehead cities of Fort William-Port Arthur.

Meanwhile, the two young hold-up men had burned their hats, masks and gloves and made preparations to flee to Winnipeg. That evening they took a taxi to the Fort William railway station to catch a train. In the rotunda Constables Owin Harty and Herman Scarnati were keeping watch on departures. They converged on Vescio and Guarasel and asked them their destination and if they had any luggage. When Vescio replied that they had two suitcases in a locker, Harty asked him to produce them.

Two suitcases were taken from a nearby locker. When Harty tried to open the smaller of the two he found it locked. After producing the key from his pocket, Vescio nervously told the officers that they would find something inside the suitcase that did not belong to him. Inside was the loaded Browning automatic, serial number CH-9847. The Port Arthur police had caught the Palm Dairy robbers. Later, at the Vescio home, police found 156 rounds of nine-millimetre ammunition.

Thirteen days later, on July 12, Magistrate Arthur Russell sentenced Michael Vescio to three years in the penitentiary for his part in the hold-up. His young accomplice, Guarasel, was given a lighter sentence of two years in the reformatory. Appearing for Vescio in the Port Arthur courtroom was the Hon. E.J. McMurray. The Winnipeg lawyer had no inkling that he would shortly be retained by the Vescio family to defend "Mickey" on far more serious charges.

Vescio himself had a premonition that the Browning automatic in the possession of the police had placed him in danger of being charged with murder. Shortly after he was arrested on the robbery charge, he asked if the gun would be sent to Toronto to be checked. He quickly added that he was asking because the provincial police had once seized a rifle from him and they had sent it to Toronto.

Port Arthur's Chief Constable George Taylor had no intention of sending the automatic to Toronto. But, as he looked at the weapon handed to him by Constable Harty, something clicked in his mind. Reaching into his desk, Chief Taylor removed the confidential memorandum sent out by the Winnipeg police over a year earlier. The next morning, he contacted Chief MacIver to tell him they had a Browning nine-millimetre automatic. He added that it had been taken from a robbery suspect who had a book in his pocket containing the names and addresses of several Winnipeg boys. MacIver asked Taylor to test fire three shots from the Browning and send them to the RCMP Crime Detection Laboratory in Regina.

On July 19, Sergeant Mason Rooke phoned MacIver with the news: he had made a positive identification. It was the gun used in the Winnipeg murders. Tough guy Vescio had made the fatal mistake of not disposing of the gun that gave him such a feeling of power.

Chapter Seven

A Moving Rope

The small public gallery in the courtroom at the Rupert Avenue police station was crowded on October 8, 1947, when the preliminary hearing of evidence against Vescio for the murder of George Smith began. Over the next three days, hundreds of the curious had to be turned away as 38 Crown witnesses took the stand.

At the press table, reporters operated in shifts. Each man would sit in the court furiously scribbling notes for about 20 minutes. He would then be relieved by a second reporter before rushing to the press room to batter out a "take" on the rickety old typewriters. Just before the afternoon deadline, and at the close of the day's session, the senior reporter would assemble the takes and write a comprehensive lead paragraph. It was then rushed to the city room for a final edit and to be typeset. It was an era when all murder trials were reported in great detail, and the Vescio case got the full treatment. Few details of the evidence were overlooked in the columns of copy that dominated the pages of the daily newspapers.

The most sensational evidence came on the second day, when Detective Inspector David Nicholson read a statement by Vescio on the day he was brought from Stony Mountain Penitentiary to the Winnipeg police station. Full details of the "confession" appeared on the front pages under lurid headlines, an action that would earn an editor a contempt of court charge today. Given the emphasis placed on the rights of the accused today, a judge might well rule for an acquittal under such circumstances. Fifty years ago, however, magistrates and judges were not worried about such sensitivities, as defence counsel Harry Walsh would learn.

In his statement, Vescio told police of going for a walk in the rain on the night George Smith was killed. He claimed that he bought a bottle of whisky and sat in a park (St. James Park, now Vimy Ridge Memorial Park) on Portage Avenue near the Home Street United Church, and drank almost half the bottle. Later, he said, he accosted a boy on Home Street and after threatening him with a gun, took him down the lane between Home and Arlington Streets to a house under construction.

"As I walked across the land, I slipped on some wet clay…I had my hand on his shoulder… He started to run when I slipped, ripping his clothes off… I lost my balance and slipped on the clay and the gun went off. I went up and touched him and felt blood on his back… I dragged him to the road. I had intended to take him to his house and leave him on the porch, but the sound of someone coming and a dog barking scared me."

Four days after being committed for jury trial on the charge of murdering George Smith, Vescio was back in the police courtroom as the preliminary evidence began on the second murder charge. As in the Smith case, a statement by Vescio describing the death of Roy McGregor was read to the court. This time the *Free Press* was slightly more circumspect, telling its readers that the "alleged" confession electrified the courtroom. Despite that slight bow to legal propriety by the addition of "alleged," the entire statement was printed almost word for word.

Vescio told of meeting young McGregor and telling him he wanted to show him something in the coal yard. "I showed him the gun…he thought it was a toy. I was going to show him how it worked…I shot off a round and then I shot off a few more… I saw him fall… I didn't know how many bullets he had in him… I knew the bullets were in him… I started to drag him… I was getting blood all over my clothes… He seemed to be dead, so I carried him to the coal bin… When I got to the house, I noticed my clothes were covered with blood. I had the clothes cleaned at the Fort Rouge Cleaners quite a while after."

Vescio was committed for jury trial on October 17, on the charge of murdering Roy McGregor. With the Fall Assizes scheduled to open four days later, Crown counsel O.M.M. Kay declined to speculate when Vescio might face a jury. "I honestly can't say right now when he will stand trial. It depends on a number of factors, not the least of which is the lengthening of the evidence."

Harry Walsh, who had put up a spirited defence despite the damning evidence put forward by the Crown, confidently predicted that it would not be necessary to ask for a traverse to the spring assizes: "Since the deposition will not be ready for the Fall Assizes." The trial would be automatically postponed, he said. As earlier set out, that expectation was short-lived. When Vescio was brought to the arraignment of the assizes on October 21, Crown Counsel C.W. Tupper said he was ready to proceed on both charges.

Walsh objected, asking that the trial be traversed to the next assize. He would need two or three months to prepare the defence and would not get a copy of the deposition until the day the trial was to begin. Meanwhile, he would be engaged in the Deacon defence. Also, he might want to seek a change of venue and have Vescio face a jury in another judicial district.

There was considerable truth in Walsh's contention that "the reprehensible course of conduct in reporting by the press from the time Vescio was arrested and right through to the preliminary hearings, predicated against selecting an unbiased jury in Winnipeg." (I admit with regret to being one of the principle sinners.) With equal validity, he added that the course of action prejudicial to the fair trial of the accused by the press had been aided and abetted by the chief of police.

Presiding over the arraignment, Mr. Justice W.J. Major was

having none of that. Acidulously pointing out that the defence had lots of opportunity to make the request since the time Vescio was first charged, he told Walsh that he didn't have to wait for committal to raise the objections. After reserving decision overnight, Major read a prepared statement the following day. Incomprehensibly, he absolved the press of any wrongdoing and added: "It has not been suggested here that these reports of the preliminary were untrue or unfair. The newspapers were strictly within the limits of the law." However, he said, it was unfortunate that such widespread publicity had been given the case, and the police authorities could not be excused for their course of conduct regarding the confession.

Stung by the reproach, Chief MacIver issued a statement the following day. Ignoring the fact that in the first flush of enthusiasm following the charging of Vescio, he had given out a written press release saying that Vescio had confessed to both murders, the chief said the press had "obtained their knowledge of the statements concerned by attending at the preliminary hearings."

As related in a previous chapter on the Deacon trials, Walsh withdrew from the defence and the court appointed John L. Ross to defend Vescio. Ross, a large, bumbling man who had a habit of sucking on an unlit pipe, thereby causing a small dribble of spittle to run down his chin, accepted the appointment over the objections of the Vescio family. Announcing the appointment of Ross, Major said he had been in touch with Walsh through an intermediary, telling him he would increase the time before trial by one week, but that Walsh still declined to act unless the trial was traversed.

Setting Vescio's trial date for November 17, Mr. Justice Major assured Ross: "Every opportunity will be given you to prepare an adequate defence." In retrospect that assurance was a hollow one. The newspaper stories arising from the dramatic clash between Walsh and Major had further predicated against hope of choosing an unbiased jury. Even with the extension of the trial date by one week, there was no hope that Ross could prepare a proper defence. The outcome of the trial was a foregone conclusion from the outset.

Vescio's two sisters and a brother, who came to Winnipeg to attend the trial, had still not given up hope of having McMurray and his partner Walsh conduct the defence. The result was that when the trial opened, McMurray was in the court accompanied by Vescio's sisters. When Crown Counsel O.M.M. Kay asked that Vescio be arraigned for trial, McMurray rose at the counsel table: "I am appearing on behalf of the accused, retained by his family."

Chief Justice E.K. Williams, resplendent in his violet robe and scarlet gun sash, was icily correct: "I am always pleased to see you appear in this court Mr. McMurray, but I am afraid that is not possible. I cannot recognize you in that capacity. Mr. Ross has been appointed to the defence some three-and-a-half weeks back."

"May I then be allowed to submit the nature of my appearance m'lord."

"You may not Mr. McMurray. My ruling is clear."

"I am perforce bound to bow to your ruling," said McMurray, who then rose and left the court.

The court clerk rose to face Vescio in the prisoner's box: "Are you ready for your trial?"

In a low voice Vescio replied: "No sir."

Ignoring the prisoner in the box, Williams turned to Ross at the counsel table: "Mr. Ross, are you ready to proceed?"

"That was the accused's answer my lord; not mine."

"You are ready to proceed then Mr. Ross?"

"I am my lord."

Ross had indicated when appointed that he might seek a change of venue to another judicial district. That appeared forgotten. The jury panel was called and selection of a jury began. Strangely, C.F. Painter, the juror whose illness necessitated restarting Deacon's second trial, was again chosen. The trial came to an abrupt halt on the third day, when Painter again became ill suffering a coronary occlusion. The jury was discharged, another chosen, and the trial began again.

When the new trial got under way, the Vescio case was forced off the front pages for the first time. The *Free Press* moved it all the way back to page 13. On Thursday, November 20, 1947, the complete front page was given over to the wedding of Princess Elizabeth to Lieutenant Phillip Mountbatten of the Royal Navy. A headline trumpeted: "World Troubles Forgotten. Royal Wedding News Fills Papers." Over the next three days, coverage of the Vescio trial was relegated to the inside pages.

That changed on November 25, when an eight-column headline appeared on the front page: "Vescio Found Guilty." The story beneath began: "Michael Angelo Vescio, aged 22, Tuesday morning was found guilty of the murder of 13-year-old Robert Smith by an assize court jury which was retired for 35 minutes before bringing in its verdict. Vescio was immediately sentenced by the presiding judge, Chief Justice E.K. Williams, Court of King's Bench, to be hanged on February 18."

With his hands folded in front of him, Vescio had taken the sentence calmly. Asked if he had anything to say before sentence was passed, he looked up and said quietly: "I have nothing your honour." Only the sobbing of his sister, Mrs. Mario Bernardi, could be heard in the courtroom.

Vescio had remained strangely unmoved throughout the trial. He showed little or no interest in the proceedings; sitting quietly as though removed from the circumstances surrounding him. At recesses and breaks in the trial, he invariably reached for a cigarette and then sat chain-smoking in the dock until the break was over. After the sentence was passed, he remained impassive as he was escorted from the courtroom, again lighting a cigarette.

Chief Justice Williams had finished his charge to the jury at 11:25 a.m. At the press table we predicted that they would be back before noon. The ballistics evidence presented by Sergeant Rooke and the statement by Vescio to the police, left little doubt about his guilt. In his final submission to the jury, Kay delivered a damning analysis of the evidence to show that Vescio had shot young Smith when he broke loose and tried to flee. Arguing that it would take two hands to hold a boy who was struggling, Kay continued: "Where was Vescio's gun at this time? It was in his pocket. It had to be drawn deliberately, cocked deliberately, and the safety catch taken off before it could be fired. Why did he fire? It's quite apparent. The boy was getting away. He didn't have far to run home. When he got there the police would be notified. There would be a hue and cry. The police would search the district. One thought only was in Vescio's mind. The boy must not get home. So, the gun was fired."

Ross, who at best had conducted a desultory defence, had little to go on. The opening lines of his 20-minute address to the jury had more of self vindication than a defence of his assigned client. Saying he was not asking for any sympathy for Vescio for anything that happened in the first days of the trial, he referred to the motion made by Walsh for time, then declared: "He has had a fair trial." He then asked for a manslaughter verdict, based on Vescio's statement that he had been drinking and that the boy had been accidentally shot.

Following the conviction, the second charge of murdering Roy McGregor was traversed pending final disposition of the Smith case.

Two days after Christmas, Harry Walsh filed an appeal against the conviction and sentencing. He charged that Mr. Justice Major had erred in failing to adjourn the trial to the next assize in order that a proper defence could be prepared, and in order that "the adverse and prejudicial publicity might be eradicated from the memories of jurymen." Walsh also claimed a miscarriage of justice because Vescio was not given the benefit of counsel of his own choice, and that Chief Justice Williams erred in failing to permit McMurray to appear on behalf of Vescio and was refused a hearing.

Other points of appeal were: that Vescio had advised the trial judge he was not ready for trial, but Williams made no enquiry as to why he was not ready; that John L. Ross indicated to the court that he would seek a change of venue, but no application was made; that Vescio asked that a witness be brought from Verdun, Quebec, but his request was overridden by Ross; that the defence of insanity was never raised or presented, and that Chief Justice Williams removed the question of manslaughter from the jury by saying there was no doubt that Robert Smith was murdered.

Pending hearing of the appeal, Vescio was granted a stay of execution to April 16, 1948. When hearing on the appeal opened March 31, Ross appeared in court to enter an objection. Claiming that certain of the grounds of appeal were an attack upon himself, Ross asked that they be struck from the record. The court merely ruled that as an interested party, he could remain in the court during the hearing if he wished. He did not.

Two weeks later, the appeal court rejected the appeal in a split three-to-two decision. Chief Justice McPherson and Justices Richards and Coyne found there had been no substantial miscarriage of justice and denied the appeal. J.E. Adamson and A.K. Dysart were of different minds. Dysart ruled that the choice of counsel was for the accused himself and rejecting the application of McMurray in advance of argument, denied the impartiality of the court. He added: "Chief Justice Williams says that the accused was ably defended by Mr. Ross. In my opinion, the defence was noticeably lacking in several respects. I can attribute it only to a lack of co-operation with the accused. It was not the defence of the accused."

Adamson declared Williams had improperly held that McMurray had no standing in the case, and had unlawfully barred him from acting. "This is not the kind of technical error that can be overlooked. The right of the accused to have counsel of his own choice is one of the rights of the democratic state. It is the difference between this state and a police state. My conclusion is that there has been a mistrial."

Vescio was again granted a stay of execution, this time to November 19 while Walsh carried the case to the Supreme Court in Ottawa. There were no reservations among the five judges of the Supreme Court. After listening to arguments from Walsh and Kay over four days in early October, they unanimously refused to grant a new trial. In a written judgement delivered on November 2, Mr. Justice Rand said that "the unchallengeable facts are so convincing and conclusive that it would seem a mockery of the practical administration of justice to require their repetition in a new trial." Justices Kerwin and Kellock concurred.

Mr. Justice Taschereau while declaring that it is a fundamental principle of criminal law that choice of counsel is the choice of the accused himself, submitted that Vescio had accepted Ross as his counsel after Walsh withdrew. "By his [Vescio's] conduct, the accused ratified the choice which he now says was forced upon him."

Mr. Justice Locke offered the same view and declared that Walsh had adequate time to get ready for the trial. "It cannot be seriously contended that twenty-four days were not ample time for counsel to prepare the defence. In my opinion, there can be no well founded criticism of the course followed by Mr. Justice Major in making the services of Mr. Ross available to the prisoner and directing the trial to proceed twenty-four days after that date, or by Chief Justice Williams in accepting the answer of Mr. Ross on November 17 that the defence was ready and directing that the trial proceed."

Three days after the Supreme Court decision was handed down, and with only two weeks left in his own life, Vescio for the second time heard the reverberating crash as the trap was released in the execution chamber next door to his cell. An ill-starred extra-marital affair had led 33-year-old Clarence J. Richardson to the gallows. On August 17, 1948, Chief Justice Williams had placed the black cloth on his head and sentenced Richardson to be "hanged by the neck until you are dead." In the silence that followed achievement of that directive, Vescio rolled over and went back to sleep.

Given the atrocity of Vescio's crime, there was little hope for commutation by the federal cabinet. On the morning of November 18, 1948, Sheriff Kyle received word that the execution was to proceed. Late that night I was back at Headingley Jail for the second time in two weeks. Unlike the sparse number of witnesses at the Deacon and Richardson hangings, there was standing room only in the waiting room beside the warden's office. It seemed that half the Winnipeg detective department was on hand to see the man who committed what they called "the most atrocious crime ever committed on the North American continent," go to his death. Nearly 50 of us made the pilgrimage through the silent prison corridors to the execution chamber before 1 a.m. on November 19.

Over the year-and-a-half that he spent in Headingley Jail, Vescio remained impassive to his surroundings. He ate what was placed in front of him without complaint and slept undisturbed. His days passed reading western and detective novels and comic books, and playing cribbage with his guards, who taught him the game. During the last week, he confessed to the shooting of both boys, describing the killings in detail and boasting that he always carried a gun. He remained confident to the last that his sentence would be commuted, but showed no emotion when told that his appeal for clemency had been denied. Up to 8 p.m. on the final night, he played cribbage with his guard.

At 11 p.m. the prison padre, Father C. Ryan, Vescio's confessor, went to the condemned cell and remained with the doomed man. They were later joined by another Catholic priest, Father O'Brien. The "tough guy" maintained his bravado to the last. When the hangman entered the cell, Vescio stood up. Taking a cigarette from his lips, he turned and butted it as the executioner moved to bind his arms behind his back.

At precisely 1 a.m., Vescio entered the execution chamber unsupported, glanced quickly around and then walked steadily to the trapdoor beneath the scaffold. Some said he was whistling. Others said his lips were puckered but no sound was coming from them. All I could hear was the intonation of the last rites by Father Ryan advancing before him. Less than 30 seconds later as Father Ryan chanted; "Jesus mercy; mercy my Jesus," Vescio dropped through the trap.

For almost a minute Father Ryan continued reading the last rites, and the crowded chamber remained hushed. But, I had been watching the rope. So had Sheriff Kyle. It was moving. Ashen-faced, Kyle moved forward, glanced down through the open trap, then turned to block the top of the stairway leading down into the pit. I knew what was happening. Vescio was strangling out of sight below us.

It was an eventuality that the hangman had feared. The previous day he had been faced with a dilemma in determining the length of drop needed to cleanly snap the condemned man's neck. During his stay in prison, the slim, slight-boned, five-foot-five Vescio had ballooned into a caricature of his former self. He gained 40 pounds and was a soft, pudgy 156 pounds with puffed cheeks and drooping jowls. Foreseeing that if he dropped his victim too far the head might come off, the hangman had erred on the safe side. The result was that Vescio's neck had not snapped.

Nauseated and shaking, I cannot recall how long Murray blocked the stairway with arms outstretched. It seemed like an eternity, and I should have had the presence of mind not to go downstairs after he stood aside. I was sorry I did. Shortly after we went down, I was startled to see Father O'Brien step forward, tear the black hood from the face of the still suspended body and anoint the forehead. I looked away. The twisted and discoloured features confirmed all too clearly that Vescio had strangled. At 1:17 a.m. Dr. Roy Martin, the prison physician, pronounced him dead and the body was lowered.

To those final minutes, I had been strangely unmoved. There had been the same grim, foreboding atmosphere in the prison, but I, with most of those who crowded the execution chamber, could muster little sympathy or compassion for a man who would sexually attack a young boy and then snuff out his victim's life simply to avoid being apprehended. I had even expressed the opinion that I would have no compunction about hanging him myself.

I have long since regretted those feelings. There can be no doubt that Vescio was guilty of the most abhorrent of crimes, and that if he had remained at large and undetected, might have killed again. In retrospect however, it is certain that in our haste to extract blind vengeance we did not grant him a fair trial. As long as the death penalty remained on the statute books, the possibility existed that the same passions might lead to equal haste to expunge the life of an innocent person.

Francis Bacon expressed it eloquently when he said: "Revenge is a wild kind of justice, which the more man's nature runs to, the more ought law to weed it out."

Chapter Eight

Once Too Often

Stella Richardson's married life was sorely tried. Her husband, Clarence George Richardson, was an unimpressive little man of 126 pounds with sandy hair, a sallow complexion and a slouching carriage. But, behind that unprepossessing exterior lay the appetite of a Lothario with an egotistic view of himself as a sexual athlete. To satisfy that appetite, Clarence Richardson would cheat on his young wife, deceive his best friend and lie to both of them. Stella, who married Clarence Richardson while she was still a schoolgirl, twice began divorce proceedings, then forgave him. In the end, Richardson's infidelities led him to the gallows at Headingley Jail, and Stella stood by him throughout his trial for the sake of their nine-year-old son.

Richardson's transgressions culminated on New Year's Day 1948, on a lonely, windswept section of St. James Street on the border of west Winnipeg. On January 2, 19-year-old Tony Miguez drove his truck north on St. James Street after a long Saturday hauling garbage for the municipality of St. James. He had just remarked to his helper, 15-year-old Watson Robinson, that he would be glad to get home for supper, when he noticed a mound of snow surrounding a small black object just west of the road.

Slowing the truck, Miguez saw what appeared to be a trail of blood leading from the road across the snow-filled ditch. Thinking it might be a dog that had been struck by a car, he brought the truck to a stop and his helper walked over to investigate. Robinson gave the black object a tentative kick, then backed away startled, as an overshoe and a leg sheathed in a silk stocking emerged from the dislodged snow. Within moments the truck was racing to the St. James police station.

St. James and Winnipeg police were on the scene when the provincial coroner, E.K. Vann, arrived at 5:20 p.m. He found the body of a woman, her face partly exposed, lying on her back with her feet protruding from the drifted snow. The head had been battered by savage blows with a blunt object. Nearby lay a ball-peen hammer with a broken handle.

A search at the morgue revealed no identification on the partly frozen body. It was that of a heavyset woman of 140 pounds, judged to be in her late twenties. She was dressed inexpensively in a blue overcoat, brown skirt and red jacket, underneath which were two pink sweaters. In hopes of finding some inscription to aid in establishing the identity of the murdered woman, Detective George Young removed a wedding ring, an engagement ring bearing one tiny diamond and a cheap wristwatch from the body. (I found the rings and watch, still unclaimed 40 years later, in the Court of King's Bench pocket at the Manitoba Archives Building and turned them over to an archivist.)

Finding nothing on the rings or the back of the watch, Young took the watch apart. Inside the back of the case were scratched the letters "McK" and some numbers. Shortly afterwards Young and an employee of McKinneys Jewellers paid a late Saturday night visit to the downtown jewellery store. In the watch repair department they found the number "850" scratched inside. The watch had been assigned to a repair for a Mrs. "Barty" of 543 Pacific Avenue in Winnipeg's north end.

At 12.30 a.m. Sunday morning, Young and his partner knocked on the door at 543 Pacific. The landlady, Mrs. W.J. Duke, sleepily answered the detective's questions. No, there was no Barty there, but Mr. and Mrs. William Varty lived on the second floor with their two children. There, an awakened William Varty told Young that his wife had left home Friday evening to help a friend move. They would probably find her at the home of a Mrs. Wilson, he said. He was asked to dress and accompany the officers to the police station.

While William Varty was undergoing further questioning, detectives awakened and questioned friends and neighbours of the Varty's. Over the next two hours, they made a positive identification of the body as that of 28-year-old Alberta Ann Varty and learned that she was having an extra-marital affair with Clarence Richardson.

A shaken Varty was told at 3 a.m. that his wife was dead, and the line of questioning abruptly changed. Did he know a man named Richardson who once worked for Western Messenger and now operated a truck of his own as Red Arrow Transfer? Yes he did. He had known him for about 18 years. Had Richardson ever been out with his wife? Yes, about four years ago. Had Richardson been out with his wife lately? No, he had not.

As gently as possible, the officers told William Varty that his wife had been seeing Richardson on a steady basis, and she was two to three months pregnant. At 6:15 a.m., the shocked and grieving husband was driven home.

Meanwhile, Sergeant of Detectives Clarence Anderson and Detective David Morris arrested 33-year-old Clarence Richardson at his home at 543 Trent Avenue in the Winnipeg suburb of East Kildonan. Just over 12 hours after discovery of the unidentified body in the snowdrift, Winnipeg police laid a charge of murder against Richardson.

Over the following 12 hours, Richardson made two statements to police. In the first, he told police that he and William Varty had been friends since they were 17 or 18 years old, but that Varty moved away from his district and they became separated. The friendship was renewed after they both married and visits were exchanged. Richardson admitted that he and Mrs. Varty had become intimate and met when he was home on leave while in the army during the war. His wife had learned about it and trouble had resulted. He had not seen Mrs. Varty until about six weeks previously, when she and her husband visited the Richardson home. He added that he had driven to Selkirk, a town north of Winnipeg, the previous Friday and on the way home he thought he might have seen Mrs. Varty. She was helping a taxi driver push a taxi that was stalled in snow beside the highway, he said.

The statement claimed that he had mentioned it to his wife on arriving home, and she had phoned the Varty home the next day to enquire about it. His wife told him that Mrs. Varty had gone out the night before and had not returned. "She mentioned that Mrs. Varty had been going out with some fellow from a taxi company, but she was not sure if it was still going on," said Richardson.

The second statement, made to Inspector of Detectives David Nicholson at 3 p.m. January 4, told a different story. Richardson admitted that he had taken Mrs. Varty with him to Selkirk on January 2. He said she told him she was in trouble with some man, that she was pregnant, and asked if he knew someone who could "fix her up." After telling how he had picked her up in suburban Elmwood at 7 p.m., the statement suddenly switched:

We parked on St. James Street that night. She threatened to expose everything. I saw red. I remembered wrestling with her. I couldn't afford the scandal. My married life is on a string now, and I don't remember anything after that. I was mad and all nervous and upset.

That same afternoon William Varty, distraught and confused, cast his mind back three-and-a-half years to late June 1944. Walking into the bedroom, he opened a drawer and withdrew an envelope. Opening it, he dropped some torn scraps of paper on the dresser. As though working on a jigsaw puzzle, he began to patiently assemble the pieces into their original form. The next day, he handed the pieces to the police. In the hands of a prosecuting attorney that letter created a ripple of shocked embarrassment in a crowded courtroom at the Summer Assizes. In an era when a more rigid code of morality prevailed, it revealed Richardson to the jury as a cheating lecher.

William Varty found the letter in his wife's drawer. Written by his boyhood friend Richardson, who he knew as "Carl," the letter had been mailed from Red Deer, Alberta, where Richardson was stationed in the Canadian army. It was addressed to Ann Varty, using her nickname "Bertie." In it Richardson told "Dearest Bertie" that he had received her letter of July 22, and that he would be coming home on furlough the evening of July 31. Arranging a tryst on his arrival, Richardson asked her to rent a room at a small hotel and to "be ready, as I am ready." The letter then detailed in lewd and lurid terms what Richardson was longing to enact with Bertie. Ending with protestations of love, the letter was signed: "Carl. The best little fucker you ever had."

It was while Ann Varty was fulfilling Richardson's fantasies at that assignation that her husband found the letter. Returning home, she was confronted with the evidence of her unfaithfulness. Richardson meanwhile had gone home to his wife who, all unsuspecting, informed him that they had been invited to dinner the next evening with his old friend Bill Varty and his wife.

It was a tense dinner with Ann Varty remaining noticeably quiet while her husband appeared agitated. After dinner, Bill Varty could contain himself no longer. Rushing from the room, he returned with the letter and handed it to Stella Richardson. She gasped as she read it, then in the strained atmosphere tried to laugh it off. The dinner party ended abruptly. Shortly afterwards Mrs. Richardson began divorce proceedings, but became reconciled with her husband when he was posted overseas. Her forbearance was tried again when Richardson became involved with a German girl while serving overseas. On his return home, she again forgave him and once more suspended divorce proceedings.

Following the disastrous dinner party, Bill Varty forgave his wife and decided to burn the evidence of her infidelity. After tearing the offensive letter into pieces he hesitated. Then, instead of consigning the pieces to the fire, he placed them in an envelope and hid it away for the next three-and-a-half years.

Defending Richardson against the damning indictment of his moral character in the letter and other evidence was S. Hart Green, a volatile and excitable lawyer of the old school of courtroom histrionics. Hart Green, who most often appeared in the court as a prosecutor on federal drug and narcotics offences, was retained by Stella Richardson to defend her husband. Richardson was committed for jury trial on January 28 following the evidence of 28 witnesses at the preliminary hearing.

Three weeks later, Richardson was arraigned at the opening of the Spring Assizes. The presiding judge, Mr. Justice W.J. Donovan, had a different view from that of his brother judge W.J. Major as to what constituted adequate time to prepare a defence. At the request of Hart Green, he traversed the Richardson trial to the Summer Assizes. Recall that Major's refusal of a like request only four days after completion of the preliminary hearing in the Vescio case resulted in Harry Walsh retiring from the defence. Blindfolded justice was not always even-handed, even in matters of life and death.

His face pale and his shoulders slumped, Richardson whispered a plea of not guilty when his trial opened before Chief Justice E.K. Williams on May 25, 1948. The assize sitting was unique since there were two murder charges to be heard that resulted from hammer slayings. Mrs. Helen Lavoie, a 36-year-old nurse, would appear before W.J. Major in the same courtroom at the end of the Richardson trial. On March 3, she crushed the skull of her 69-year-old mother-in-law with repeated blows of a hammer in their home in the rural Manitoba town of Letellier.

Faced with Richardson's statement to police and production

of the reassembled letter of 1944, Hart Green had little room for manoeuvre. The defence fought desperately to keep the second statement to police from entering the record. Arguing that Richardson was kept incommunicado, Hart Green alleged his client had been denied the services of a lawyer until detectives extorted a statement from him by threats and promises. In a four-and-a-half hour trial within a trial, Hart Green called lawyer L.A. Seipp, Inspector Nicholson and then Richardson to the stand with the jury retired.

Seipp testified that he was retained by Stella Richardson shortly after the arrest and had gone to the police station at 2 p.m. on January 4. When he asked to see Richardson, Nicholson replied that his men were with him and he could not see his client for a couple of hours. When he protested that he might want to give Richardson some advice, Nicholson still refused permission to see him, Seipp said. He was not told there was a charge against Richardson and was not allowed to see him until 6 p.m. By that time the statement had been taken. When Nicholson said he could not remember Seipp coming to see him Hart Green, whose normal voice was a high-pitched rasp, almost screamed: "Since Inspector Nicholson has been chief of detectives for Winnipeg, there have been confessions for almost every murder."

Chief Justice Williams was not swayed. With his customary icy preciseness, he noted that Richardson, while on the stand during the test of admissibility, had admitted that the statement was true. "The statement of the accused in the box on this confession, as I am calling it, casts an entirely different light on the credibility of this witness." Williams added that he had studied Richardson's demeanour and did not believe his statement that Nicholson had told him they had evidence against him before getting the statement. Hart Green's argument that the issue was not a case of whether the statement was true or untrue, but the manner in which it was obtained, was of little avail. Williams stood firm. The jury was recalled, and the "confession" was entered as an exhibit.

Only one chance remained for Richardson. On the fifth day of the trial, Hart Green called the accused man to the stand. Disclaiming responsibility for Ann Varty's pregnancy, he told the jury that she had threatened to throw the blame on him and break up his marriage.

> She didn't care. She said that if her married life was to break up, she would break up mine and we could be back together again... We sat there for two or three minutes. Then she got out of the truck and went around the back. I got out and followed her. She was shouting, swearing and screaming and hysterical. I grabbed her and started to shake her. She got hysterical and put her hand on my chest and pushed me back, and going backwards I struck my head on the back of the truck. That's the last thing I remember until I found myself going over Redwood Bridge. There is nothing I can recall between then and the time I struck my head.

Richardson told the jury he had decided to change his first statement after Nicholson told him they had a witness who had identified Ann Varty's body as that of a woman who was in his truck when he drove to Selkirk. "When he told me that, I took it to understand they knew they had me where they wanted me." After saying he had let her out of the truck on Main Street at Redwood Avenue, he had switched his story when Nicholson told him "there's a manslaughter charge in this province and it's possible you may get off with manslaughter."

Richardson also said he had made a mistake in his statement when he said his married life was on a string. "My married life was beginning to get along good. I had no trouble with my wife after I got back from overseas, and I was afraid Mrs. Varty was going to upset my married life."

Then, in a move aimed at convincing the jury that Richardson had been forgiven his marital transgressions, Stella Richardson was called as a defence witness. While small and pretty, her face bore a strange pallor of an almost grey transparency. At the press table we attributed it to the strain of the trial, but there was a deeper underlying cause.

If the defence strategy had been to gain the sympathy of the jury, Stella Richardson's appearance may have backfired and weakened her husband's defence that he had suffered a blackout after striking his head. Under cross-examination, Crown Counsel Charles Tupper drew out the damaging evidence that, on his return home January 2, her husband told her he thought he had seen Mrs. Varty beside the road on the way to Selkirk, and that he had not complained of any injury to his head.

Chief Justice Williams made pointed reference to Stella Richardson's testimony in his charge to the jury: "There was no mention of striking his head in the statement to police. Then, when he gets home, he tells his wife a concocted story. Why? You will have to test and see if he told the truth in the box. Assuming he did slip and hit his head; did he have a concussion? You will bear in mind that he went home and never told his wife about it, and went about his work the next day."

While giving the jury the choice of bringing in a verdict of murder or manslaughter, Williams made his own opinion abundantly clear: "There can be no doubt that Mrs. Varty was murdered. It would seem to be clear she was murdered about midnight the second of January." He also defused any chance that the defence of provocation might succeed: "It has been stated judicially that all murders, except those committed for gain, are committed after provocation of some sort. It is only when provocation consists of a wrongful act or insult of such a nature as to deprive an ordinary man of his power of self-control, and he acts upon it before there is time for passion to cool, that a killing can become manslaughter. The mental make-up of the accused is not to be taken into consideration therefore in deciding if there has been provocation."

It didn't take long. The jury retired at 11:18 a.m., adjourned for lunch at 12 noon and returned with the verdict one minute after the noon recess was over. Guilty of murder as charged. Richardson took the verdict calmly, and after Chief Justice Williams sentenced him to be hanged at Headingley Jail on August 17, swept his hand across his forehead and sat down.

In the silent courtroom, Stella Richardson rose and walked to the prisoner's box to speak with her husband before the sheriff's officers led him away. Short though his remaining life span was, hers was to prove shorter. Seven days later she collapsed in their small home and died of a brain haemhorrage.

Prolonged beyond the five days allotted to it on the court calendar, the Richardson trial had delayed that of Helen Lavoie which began the next day in the same courtroom before Mr. Justice W.J. Major. Three days later she stepped from the prisoner's box, free to return home to her husband and two children in Letellier. As in the Richardson case, the victim's head had been pulverized by repeated blows of a ball-peen hammer. RCMP officers were summoned to the Lavoie home to investigate a family quarrel and found Mrs. Lavoie baking bread in the kitchen. After leaving the house to phone police, she had returned and cleaned up the home. But, in a corner of the living room, the body of her mother-in-law, Celina Manseau, lay crumpled in a bloody heap. Six-and-a-half years of living in the same house, in almost constant conflict, had ended in tragedy.

A contention by Harry Walsh that the 86-pound Mrs. Lavoie had acted in self defence when attacked by her 160-pound mother-in-law, resulted in complete acquittal. Juries always showed reluctance to convict women on the major charge while capital punishment was in effect. And while given the alternative of manslaughter, the jury took less than two hours to bring in an acquittal on all counts. In the eyes of juries, there was a wide moral divide between marriage infidelity and a family dispute.

Four months later, the five judges of the Manitoba Court of Appeal gave short shrift to an argument by Hart Green that Chief Justice Williams had erred in not putting Richardson's defence of amnesia or provocation to the jury. The charge merely tried to "beat to a pulp" the defence, said Hart Green. Chief Justice McPherson read the unanimous decision of the court one week after the appeal hearing. There were several statements in the charge to the jury which, if standing by themselves, might be grounds for an appeal, said the court. However, if the charge was considered as a whole, it was a fair charge.

Richardson's only hope now lay in an appeal for clemency and commutation of the sentence to life imprisonment. The application having been made, the Remission Service began gathering the minutiae of the case and the background of the condemned man to prepare a summary for the deputy minister of justice. From the police was required "all relevant information concerning the motive for the crime, peculiarities of character, environment and antecedents."

There could be little comfort for Richardson in the report forwarded by the Winnipeg police. Without giving any background for the conclusions, the report declared: "Richardson was a shifty type, and although he had not been previously convicted of a criminal offence, the company he kept was not of the best, and he was definitely morally unsound."

Chief Justice Williams made little comment either for or against commutation. Saying that Richardson was "ably defended and tried before an intelligent jury," he concluded that he was satisfied "the jury had reached the only verdict it could have reached on proper consideration of the evidence."

Adding to the negative impact of the police and trial judge's reports was another from the Manitoba attorney-general's office. It declared there "was no outstanding feature warranting commutation." The summary from the Remission Service while admitting that a blow to the head might have diminished Richardson's capacity to kill with full intent, noted there was no evidence of the head injury when he returned home after the killing, and that he carried out his normal routine thereafter. It recommended that the sentence not be interfered with. Justice Minister Ilsley in turn passed on the report to cabinet with a recommendation of his own that was against commutation.

On October 27, 1948, the cabinet considered the case and concluded that it was unable to order interference with the sentence.

Richardson took the news calmly, though he had told visitors that he had a premonition he would be granted clemency and would not hang. Thereafter he remained stoic, ate and slept well and refused a spiritual adviser. Throughout the afternoon preceding the execution, Reverend H.S. Dodgson, a former service padre and rector of King United Church in East Kildonan, waited at the jail. But, the doomed man refused to see him.

The padre was still waiting at the jail when I arrived shortly after midnight on November 5, 1948, to cover the hanging. At the last moment a guard entered the waiting room and told Reverend Dodgson that Richardson wanted to see him. It was 12:50 a.m. In the condemned cell, Richardson told the padre; "Father, it is quite all right. I am reconciled." His sole thought was for his son, who within minutes would be an orphan, and he gave Dodgson a message to deliver to the boy.

At 1:17 a.m., the door to the execution chamber opened and Richardson walked in unaided. Betraying no emotion, he walked calmly to the raised platform beneath the scaffold without saying a word. Reverend Dodgson stood just inside the entrance to the chamber facing Richardson. As the black hood was being placed over his head, Richardson gave the padre a faint smile and winked. It was a prearranged signal for Reverend Dodgson to silently repeat the Lord's Prayer. Eighteen seconds after he had entered the chamber, Richardson dropped through the trap. At 1:28 a.m.,

Dr. Roy Martin, the jail physician, placed a stethoscope on the hanged man's chest and pronounced him dead. It had been a clean, quick execution.

When Michael Vescio walked to his death in the same chamber two weeks later, the condemned cells fell empty for the first time in two years. They would not stay empty long. The next time the lever released the trapdoors, two men would plunge to their deaths back-to-back.

Chapter Nine

Back-to-Back

After the grim silence of the Richardson hanging, where not a single word was spoken, and the postured bravado leading to Vescio's strangulation, the combined execution of Camille Allarie and William Lusanko at Headingley Jail on May 9, 1950, came as a shock.

Allarie, an illiterate farmhand charged following the apparently motiveless shooting of the farm couple for whom he worked, entered the chamber sobbing loudly and accompanied by two Roman Catholic priests reciting prayers.

Behind him came Lusanko repeating prayers intoned by a Greek Orthodox monk in a brown cassock. The victim of an indifferent upbringing by uncaring parents, Lusanko had been underfed, undereducated and underclothed. He left school at 14 to make his way in a neighbourhood described in a police report as being "low class, and populated mostly by criminals, bootleggers, and other low types of humanity." He came to this place of horror solely on the evidence of a convicted fraud artist and "stool pigeon," who shared a cell with him, gained his confidence, then took the stand as a Crown witness against him.

Three of Lusanko's accomplices in the ill-fated robbery that led him to the gallows sat in the court as free men throughout his trial, and two of them gave evidence against him as Crown witnesses. They did so with impunity because of a safeguard in our legal system that decrees that "hearsay evidence" implicating another person in a crime cannot be used against the person, or persons implicated. Hearsay evidence is defined in Webster as "evidence repeated at second hand by one who heard the actual witness relate or admit what he knew of the transaction or fact in question." In short, a confession related first-hand by one person to another can be used as evidence against the person making the confession. However, if another person, or persons, are implicated in that confession and they are not there to defend themselves against the allegations, it is not evidence against them. The law recognizes that if I confess to a crime it can be used against me, but I cannot take others down with me.

Beside the fact that Allarie and Lusanko hanged together, the cases were unique in my court reporting experience in several other respects. Both were defended by C.N. "Chaime" Kushner. In neither case was there an appeal, and they were the only two of the seven cases outlined in this book in which Chief Justice E.K. Williams did not pass the death sentences. In the case of Lusanko, it was the only trial of the seven in which the jury brought in a recommendation for mercy.

The violent passing of these two pitiful cast-offs of an uncaring society went virtually unnoticed. Winnipeg and the Red River Valley were under siege by the worst flood in this century on May 9, 1950, when Allarie and Lusanko dropped simultaneously to their doom. The sobbing and the prayers were cut off abruptly thirty seconds after they entered the execution chamber. With news of the flood crisis dominating the front pages, my report of their deaths was relegated to space deep inside the *Winnipeg Free Press.*

The temptation that led 21-year-old Bill Lusanko to the final retribution of society had its origin in May 1949, when a fire broke out in a shed behind 266 Dufferin Avenue in a shabby, derelict area of Winnipeg's north end. Cramped into the backyard with the shed was the dilapidated, unpainted shack of 65-year-old Dora Sadova. A bootlegger, she was known locally as the "cat woman" because of the half-dozen or more cats that shared her ramshackle quarters where she lived otherwise alone.

As smoke billowed from the shed, a neighbour across the lane saw the squat, heavy-set Dora Sadova trying to drag a heavy trunk from her shack and screaming for help. When the neighbour went to her aid, Dora blurted out that all her money was in the trunk and she had to get it out in case the fire spread to her home. Later, when the shed fire was contained, she confided to the neighbour that she had a husband in the United States and that they sold a house there. Her share of the sale, about $5,000, was in the trunk. Asked why she did not keep it in the bank, Mrs. Sadova said she was afraid welfare officials would learn of it and cancel her social allowance.

That revelation in a crime-ridden area where a $5,000 fortune was only a dream, may have signed the cat woman's death warrant. Casual gossip was bound to reach the wrong ears. On September 13, 1949, the body of Dora Sadova, her hands bound behind her back with adhesive tape, was found sprawled on the grimy floor of her hovel. She had died of suffocation, and the treasure-laden trunk had been ransacked.

When police came, they found evidence that the short, obese, five-foot-two, 178-pound woman might have fallen from her bed to the floor of her tiny bedroom while struggling to free herself. However, there was a pillow with what appeared to be bloodstains nearby on top of the trunk. It appeared that Dora Sadova had been in bed when somebody broke a window and entered the shack. She was wearing two cheap cotton dresses, one over the other, and her hair was braided. While there were no marks of injury on her body, there was a pool of blood beside her head. The coroner diagnosed that she had died of "obstructive asphyxiation," and the pool of blood probably resulted from bleeding at the nose. "Other than her trussed-up hands, I am quite satisfied there was no violence involved," said Dr. I.O. Fryer.

One week later, Winnipeg police detained four young men and held them for questioning. They included Bill Lusanko, 19-

year-old Henry Bender, 18-year-old Leslie Raymond Kahlian, and a 16-year-old juvenile. Charged with conspiracy to commit a robbery, Lusanko, Bender and Kahlian appeared in court the next week. Chaime Kushner, as counsel for Bender, asked that the Crown proceed with the trial on the charges, or that bail be allowed. He contended the Crown was ignoring the rights of the young men by holding them without bail and refusing to bring them to trial.

The facts were that the police did not have enough evidence to substantiate the charges. Crown prosecutor O.M.M. Kay staved off the defence demand by saying that scientific tests were being undertaken on stains found on certain clothing at the time of the arrests. His request that the young men be remanded without bail for a further week was granted.

Kushner protested, reminding Kay: "In the course of his work, my learned friend overlooks the fact that the liberty of the subject is more important than whether or not the police get a conviction." He may have protested even more vehemently had he known the lengths to which the police would go over the following weeks to get a conviction. While Bender and Kahlian were held at the Fort Rouge police station, Lusanko was placed in a cell at the central Rupert Avenue station with a stool pigeon, who became known as the mysterious "Mr. X."

Three weeks after he had been arrested on the conspiracy charge and held without bail, Lusanko was charged with the murder of Mrs. Sadova. One week later, Bender and Kahlian, still facing conspiracy charges, were released on bail of $6,000 each. Kushner was then representing all three of the young men. However, when the preliminary hearing on the murder charge against Lusanko opened on November 3, he found himself defending Lusanko alone. His other two clients had turned against their companion and were now witnesses for the prosecution. The conspiracy charges against them would be dropped.

The first inkling of the double-cross came on the first day of the preliminary hearing when Kay called Kahlian to the stand. Shocked at the sudden turn of events, Kushner asked for a short adjournment to talk to Kahlian privately. Magistrate M.H. Garton refused the request, ruling that Kushner could bring his questions out in cross-examination.

Kahlian began his self-serving testimony by saying that Lusanko came to his home in early September and asked him to "go on a job with him." He said Lusanko then showed him a house on Dufferin Avenue and told him there was a woman there who had $4,000 or $5,000. "And he asked me if I wanted to go with him, and I said I didn't want to go. And I said I wouldn't, so he said he had someone else to go with him."

A small wisp of a man with a pencil moustache set in a narrow face that widened to a broad forehead, Kushner was an experienced defence counsel with a sharp intellect. His voice rising in a sibilant hiss, he confronted Kahlian: "When did you decide to give evidence here? What made you change your mind?"

"Because I wanted to tell the truth. I have nothing to be afraid of."

"A couple of days ago you didn't want to give evidence did you?"

"No."

"What did I tell you the other day about giving evidence in court here today? Do you remember?"

"No."

"Do you remember what you told me?"

"I said I wouldn't."

"What made you change your mind now?"

"Because I had nothing to hide."

"Why didn't you tell me then you would give evidence? Who were you talking to Leslie? Just answer me. Who were you talking to?"

Shifting uneasily in the witness box, his eyes downcast to avoid those of the irate defence counsel, Kahlian finally said a detective had called him into a cruiser car the previous evening when he was out for a walk and told him the best thing he could do was tell the truth.

"Did he say that it will help you out? That the case against you might be dropped?"

"No."

There was a similar performance when Henry Bender took the stand. As in the surprise appearance of Kahlian, the Crown requested and got protection of the court for Bender who also gave a self-serving account of being approached by Lusanko to go on a job about a week before the death of Dora Sadova. "He told me there was a woman on Dufferin that was a bootlegger, and he says we can go through the window—she keeps it by a mattress someplace. I says no."

Kushner again moved in: "Who saw you since last Sunday?"

"Nobody."

"Did any police officer see you since then?"

"Well, Inspector Blow this morning."

"Was it the first time any police officer saw you since I saw you last Sunday?"

"That's correct."

"What was the conversation between you and Inspector Blow? Now I want the truth Bender."

"I am telling you the truth."

"What was the conversation between you and Blow?"

"I told him I wanted to see him."

"You sent for Blow?"

"Yes…I asked him if it would do me any harm or any good if I testified, so he said it was up to me. So I figured I had better."

If the sudden turning of his companions against Lusanko came as a shock, there was a greater one to come. The old adage that there is honour among thieves was about to be disproven in spades.

The preliminary hearing bogged down on the second day,

when Kay said that an important witness—identified only as Mr. X—could not be found. A subpoena had been drawn up, but police had not yet found him. "Normally, I would give the court a context of this missing witness' testimony…but I know the defence counsel would want to cross-examine him," said Kay.

It was over a month before the preliminary hearing resumed. Meanwhile, the Crown entered a stay of proceedings on the conspiracy to commit robbery charges against Kahlian and Bender. They were now out on bail as material witnesses in the case against Lusanko.

When the preliminary hearing reopened on December 15, the elusive Mr. X was escorted into the courtroom by police officers. He was 47-year-old Allan Cox, an ex-convict with a long string of fraud convictions dating from 1923. Arrested on a fraud charge September 26, he had been placed in a cell with Lusanko for three-and-a-half days. He was then released on his own recognizance without putting up surety. He simply assured the magistrate that he would turn up for his trial. He then disappeared and when Winnipeg police caught up with him again he was serving a four-month term in Headingley Jail.

In retrospect, it is almost beyond belief that the Crown would put forward such a corrupt source of evidence. It is even more incredible that a jury convicted and the court sentenced a man to hang on the evidence of a man who gave a commitment to obtain his own release and then disappeared. There is little doubt that, without the evidence of Allan Cox, Lusanko would not have been convicted.

With all the aplomb of a seasoned con-artist, the affable Cox related his conversations with Lusanko during their time together in the jail cell. After being placed in the cell with Lusanko, Cox tried to arrange bail. Lusanko asked him if he would do him a favour if he got out. He wanted Cox to contact Bender at either the Fort Rouge or North End police station and ask whether Bender had said anything to police, especially about a broken pane of glass in Dora Sadova's home. Cox was to return to the front of the Rupert Avenue police station and shout to Lusanko what he had learned.

While it was never disclosed in court, it does not take much imagination to guess what happened after that. Most probably Cox—who could not afford to put up bail—went to the police with a deal. If the Crown would arrange for him to be released on his own recognizance, he would pump Lusanko for further details and be a witness for the prosecution. That probability is given credence by the fact that police knew when a message would be called to Lusanko, and posted a detective in a nearby cell to listen when the messenger appeared. The code name "Judas" might have been more appropriate than "Mr. X."

Cox's evidence, outlining what Lusanko had told him over a three-day period in the jail cell, was related in an unbroken monologue. Lusanko, he said, told him that he, Harry Bender, Leslie Kahlian and his younger brother, Joe Kahlian, had been drinking homebrew on September 12, and had then gone to Dora Sadova's shack. Lusanko told him he had broken a small piece of glass from a window and opened the catch. He then crawled in and opened the door for the others. As he was opening the door, Mrs. Sadova grabbed him from behind. In the ensuing struggle, Lusanko pushed the woman onto her bed and held her by the wrist with one hand while putting the other over her mouth. Meanwhile, Bender entered and taped the struggling woman's wrists behind her back. He then began to search the trunk next to the bedroom door. Joe Kahlian went into the kitchen and began searching the dish cupboard while Leslie Kahlian stood by the door on watch. All this time, Lusanko stood by the bed with his hand over the victim's mouth to prevent any outcry. After Bender found some money, bonds and watches in the trunk, the four robbers left the shack and went to Lusanko's home. Lusanko told him Mrs. Sadova was still on the bed breathing naturally when they left.

At Lusanko's home they found they had over $300 in Canadian money, $427.89 in American money, two $1,000 bonds and two watches. The Canadian money was divided equally and Lusanko kept the American money to be exchanged and divided later. Bender took the bonds to find a buyer with the proceeds to be shared later. Lusanko kept the two watches, one a Waltham railway watch and the other a Bulova wristwatch, to be sold and the money shared.

Cox continued: "When this was over, Bill Lusanko noticed a button was missing off his jacket sleeve. He put on an army jacket, returned to the house and when he got in he found the woman lying on the floor and quite a bit of blood around her. He told me that he thought he got some blood on his army tunic sleeve. He searched for the button and couldn't find it. Later he told me if I thought that the blood on the tunic sleeve could be proved that it came from the dead woman's body. I said I thought it had...thought they could do it at the barracks where they test blood."

Answering a series of questions by Crown counsel, Cox said Lusanko had worried about the bonds and some American change in his pocket being traced by the police. Lusanko also said that, after he returned home, he cut all the buttons off the sleeves of his jacket. He noticed that the lapel had been torn in the struggle with Mrs. Sadova, and had sewn it up. He also said that, when he left the shack the second time; "the woman was on the floor and there was blood all around her and she was not breathing naturally. She was gasping for breath."

At the opening of Lusanko's jury trial, presided over by Mr. Justice W.J. Major, on February 20, 1950, Kushner said he would contest the admissibility of Cox's evidence. Therefore, no mention of it was made in Crown Counsel C.W. Tupper's outline of evidence at the outset of the trial. But, when Cox was called to the stand the next day, the expected legal battle over admissibility did not develop. Kushner had studied the legal precedents overnight, and reluctantly conceded that the most recent authorities ruled against him. Cox, in the same casual, unreserved style, again related his jail cell conversations with Lusanko. He combined them as before into an uninterrupted account.

In cross-examination, Kushner was able to stress that Lusanko was surprised when he learned that Mrs. Sadova died. He was also able to zero in on Cox's lengthy record of fraud convictions. Cox affably admitted them, but denied he had been promised any favours by the police in return for his testimony. Like Kahlian and Bender, he said he only wanted to tell the truth.

Waiting in the witness room to testify against their friend, Bender and Leslie Kahlian were basking in their new-found notoriety. They swaggered in the marble-lined corridors, cigarettes dangling from their mouths, and with wide-brimmed fedoras dented into a distinctive "Chicago block" pushed back on their heads. The hats signified membership in the Dew Drop gang, an unruly group of young thugs who hung out at the Dew Drop Inn in Winnipeg's north end.

Bender followed Cox to the witness stand. He repeated his story that Lusanko had approached him to "knock off a lady bootlegger," but said he had refused. In cross-examination he denied that he had ever been at Dora Sadova's shack. He made a bad impression on Mr. Justice Major who regarded him with grim-faced mistrust.

Leslie Kahlian made an even less favourable impression. When he swaggered into the courtroom chewing gum, Major ordered a guard to take it from him. Then, as he was taking the oath, Kahlian laughed. Major was aghast; "Why did you laugh young man? I hope you realize the significance of the oath you have taken. I remind you that you can be charged with perjury if you give false witness here." Like his companion, Kahlian denied ever being near Mrs. Sadova's shack, though Lusanko had invited him to take part in the robbery. Jail-hardened and street-wise, both of Lusanko's accomplices knew that to admit complicity in open court might lead to serious charges being laid against them. A chance of being charged with perjury was preferable to being charged with murder.

Major's antipathy to Bender and Kahlian whom he described as "accomplices whose evidence must be looked upon with a great deal of suspicion," did not prevent him from delivering a harsh charge to the jury. Outlining the law concerning the evidence of accomplices and hearsay evidence, Major said: "That is probably why Kahlian and Bender are not facing charges of murder today."

He had no reservations about believing the Crown's key witness however. Despite Cox's unsavoury background, Major told the jury that Cox had impressed him as having a good memory, and he could find no evidence that he was shaken in cross-examination. Cox, said the judge, had nothing to gain by coming to court to tell his story and in his opinion had nothing but a desire to see justice done.

Dealing with the defence, Major said he scarcely knew what to tell the jury: "I have found nothing in my notes which would indicate any defence." While giving the jury the choice of returning a verdict of either murder, manslaughter or acquittal, Major left no doubt of his own opinion as he outlined the principles of law:

"It is murder if some person willfully stops the breath of another person for the purpose of robbery and death ensues, whether or not he intends to cause death, or whether or not he knows death might ensue. If you find that the accused did stop the breath of the woman for the purpose of facilitating robbery and the woman died as a result of it, then it is murder."

Concentrating on the record of Cox, Kushner told the jury: "Fraud is a peculiar business, it calls for deception. It's a sneaking business. Cox told that story for his own freedom… If one of you gentlemen get in jail on a fraud charge, you won't be released on your own recognizance. You will have to get someone to go bond for you."

Charles Tupper, in his summary for the Crown, dissipated some of the jury's reticence to accept Cox's story by pointing to corroborating evidence. The broken glass from the window and Lusanko's grey flannel jacket with the torn and crudely sewn lapel and the buttons cut off the sleeve had been entered as exhibits. "How did Cox know about a piece of broken glass in the window, or the button being off Lusanko's coat, unless Lusanko told him?" Tupper also defused at least part of the impression left by the dubious evidence of Lusanko's obvious accomplices by saying the Crown was most anxious that other persons be charged "when evidence becomes available."

That, capped by the "hanging" charge delivered by Major, appeared to leave few doubts in the minds of the jury, despite the tainted sources of the evidence presented to them. It took less than an hour for the jury to return a verdict of guilty of murder. However, in a gesture of lingering concern, the jury added a recommendation for mercy.

Lusanko accepted the verdict calmly. Asked if he had anything to say before sentencing, he replied in a clear voice; "I'm innocent. I had nothing to do with it." He remained calm as Major sentenced him to be hanged at Headingley Jail some time between 1 a.m. and 8 a.m. on May 4, 1950.

In the front row of the courtroom, Bender and the two Kahlians were shaken. The importance of what had been at stake during the trial seemed to finally penetrated their bravado. In their twisted understanding, jail sentences were a natural, and expected, hazard of a precarious existence. A violet robed judge placing a black cloth on his head and sentencing one of their fellows to be hanged by the neck until he was dead was something different.

While no appeal was filed against the conviction and sentencing, Kushner made a personal appeal to the minister of justice in Ottawa on April 14:

"I am not entirely satisfied that the verdict is a proper one, not so much as to whether it should have been murder or manslaughter, since that is a matter of law, but as to whether Lusanko was, or was not, one of those who committed this offence. Of course, I cannot definitely state that he was not on the premises on the night in question but, from conversations which I had with two of the young men, whom the Crown suspects of having been parties to this offence, as well as conversations with others who were interested in this matter, I feel in spite of the evidence that has been produced before the jury that Lusanko may be entirely innocent. I have never written a letter to you or your department asking for commutation of the death penalty as I do not recall a case in which I was interested, in almost 20 years of practice at the Bar, when I felt so strongly about the necessity and need for commutation."

The police report forwarded to the Remission Service confined itself mainly to the facts of the case. It did not appear to be particularly against commutation, noting that the environment in which Lusanko was raised was "particularly anti-social," and that Lusanko's nominal guardian was his mother who "showed no interest in his welfare."

Many letters were sent to Ottawa by those in the community who had been associated with, or who knew, Lusanko. There was a common theme running through most of them. A former teacher wrote of his "horrendous upbringing." His family was always on relief; his father was a drunkard and treated him with great cruelty, she said. His former school principal described him as having been "treated like a dog." His mother was married four times and neglected her children. He was underfed and underclothed and had been forced to leave school at an early age, said the principal.

Other letters voiced the opinion that he and his companions were of subnormal intelligence and expressed doubts that Lusanko had taken part in the robbery, or at least that he did not commit the fatal assault. A lengthy petition was also sent to Ottawa urging commutation to life imprisonment.

That outpouring of protest appears to have been completely counter-balanced by a harsh report from the trial judge. Stressing that he found the disreputable Cox to be a believable witness, W.J. Major wrote:

"In spite of his record of convictions and the doubt created thereby as to his credibility, the man showed a remarkable memory... I formed the opinion that Cox was a truthful witness; that there was nothing in his demeanour to suggest untruthfulness, and he gave his evidence without reserve or any indication of bias... There can be no doubt that the accused is the man who held the woman's mouth and nose and that she died of asphyxiation as a result. This young man is a member of a gang of bad young men. His record shows that he has been in trouble since he was 11 years old. He and his companions are a menace to the whole neighbourhood. There is no ameliorating circumstance— beyond the fact that the accused's accomplices have not been caught—which gives any ground as a reason for the exercise of executive clemency, and I cannot recommend it."

Major's brutal assessment was a major part of the summary forwarded to the solicitor-general by the Remission Service. The report also stressed evidence which tended to corroborate the evidence of Cox and recommended against clemency.

On April 27, 1950, the cabinet ruled against commutation and decreed that the sentence of death be carried out. The date of May 4, set by Major had to be extended at the last moment when a hangman scheduled to come from Toronto was taken ill. The rotund French-Canadian "Camille," was contacted and on May 9, at 2:25 a.m., Dr. John Martin pronounced Bill Lusanko dead. Three minutes later he pronounced Camille "Bijou" Allarie dead.

One week before opening his unsuccessful defence of Lusanko, Kushner made legal history in the same courtroom when the trial of Allarie on a charge of murdering Mrs. William Delbridge opened before Mr. Justice P.J. Montague. Before the trial began,

Kushner made an unprecedented move. He asked permission of the court to address the jury and give an outline of the defence in advance of the prosecution's evidence.

After the jury had been chosen, he asked that they be retired while he made a motion to be allowed certain actions. With the jury absent, Kushner explained to the judge that it was one of those rare cases where he did not think the Crown and the defence would have any differences regarding the facts. "The same witnesses who appear for the Crown are also virtually defence witnesses, and I intend to subpoena some of the Crown witnesses for the defence." He asked permission to examine Crown witnesses as defence witnesses when they appeared to save calling them twice. He also asked permission to outline the theory of the defence immediately following the Crown's outline of evidence expected at the trial.

Arguing that Kushner should properly make his outline of the defence at the end of the prosecution's evidence, Crown Counsel W.J. Johnston declared the right of the Crown came from the common law and had never been taken away. However, if the judge thought such a proceeding would facilitate the trial, then his objection was not strenuous, although he doubted the defence had such a right.

Given the lenient attitude of the Crown, Montague granted Kushner's request, thereby setting a legal precedent.

In his outline preceding the hearing of evidence, Kushner admitted to the jury that Allarie borrowed a hunting rifle and shot his employers, Mr. and Mrs. William Delbridge, in their farm home near Poplar Point, a small hamlet 41 miles west of Winnipeg. He directed the jury to the question of intent. "Whatever happened that night, happened under such unusual conditions that the accused was not in the frame of mind to realize his actions. I ask you to concentrate so as to arrive at his frame of mind on that night. You will find later that it is the gist of the defence, whether he intended to kill anyone."

The uncontested evidence showed that Allarie, a simple-minded man with a grade three education who said he could not read or write, had worked for the Delbridge family as a farm hand for 15 years. The youngest of five children, he could not remember his parents and had been brought up by an aunt. He first went to work for William Delbridge's father and had grown up with the Delbridge children on the farm near Poplar Point. In his own words, he and William Delbridge "were just like brothers."

On September 23, a dance was held at Poplar Point to celebrate Edith Delbridge's fortieth birthday. Before dinner that evening, Allarie left to go to nearby Portage la Prairie intending to go to the dance later. Mr. and Mrs. Delbridge left the farm for the dance following dinner, taking the eldest of their five children, 13-year-old Joan, with them. The four younger children were left in the care of a neighbour. Leaving the dance about 2 a.m., they returned home and went to bed.

There was no sign of trouble at the dance. Allarie came back from Portage la Prairie and his actions throughout the evening appeared normal according to witnesses. Jean Ann Bruce of Poplar Point, said she danced every second dance with Allarie and had gone out to eat with him at the intermission. She could recall nothing unusual in his actions and said while he might have been drinking, he was not drunk. Allarie left the dance shortly after the Delbridges returned to the farm.

At 2:45 a.m., Roy Cryderman, a railway section hand living in a bunk car at Poplar Point, woke to find Allarie standing in the doorway of the car holding a match. Allarie wanted to talk, and they shared a bottle of beer Allarie had brought with him and discussed the dance. At one point Allarie asked to borrow a rifle, but Cryderman refused the request. After about ten minutes, Allarie stood up, took a 30.30 Winchester rifle from where it hung on the wall of the bunk house and walked out. In the doorway, Cryderman called out to him to return, but Allarie disappeared into the darkness.

Outside the weather-beaten, unpainted Delbridge farm-house, Allarie reached in his pocket and took out some rifle shells he had taken unnoticed from a drawer in the railway bunkhouse and loaded the rifle. Taking off his shoes, he crossed the rickety back porch and walked into the kitchen. A few minutes later two shots shattered the stillness.

Wakened by the shots, nine-year-old Clayton Delbridge heard his mother cry out "my heart," and then his father say; "Bijou, Bijou why did you shoot?" In another bedroom, Joan Delbridge was wakened by her eight-year-old sister Karen. She heard her father and mother groaning in the living room. "Dad said 'Bijou, Bijou,' then Bijou said, 'Bill, Bill, are you O.K.'"

Going toward the living room; Joan saw Allarie walking to the kitchen carrying the rifle and a flashlight. Suddenly noticing her, Allarie sat down on a couch and started to cry. Between sobs, he blurted; "Look at all your father and mother have done for me and look what I have done to them. Shall I shoot myself Joanie?" The young girl showed great presence of mind. "I said 'no put the gun down.' He didn't do it, so I said it several times and finally he put the gun down." Meanwhile, she told her brother Clayton to telephone a neighbour, but Allarie told him to go back to bed.

Rising from the couch, Allarie walked into the girl's bedroom and sat on Joan's bed crying; "I should have been hung long ago. I'm never going to see you kids again." Clayton rose again. Skirting the bodies of his parents on the living room floor he reached the phone. When the neighbours came Allarie was still sitting on the edge of Joan's bed crying. One of them picked up the rifle, took it outside and hid it in the backyard. Then he phoned the RCMP. Allarie was still crying when they locked him in a cell in Portage la Prairie.

At the trial, Joan and Clayton related the grim events of that night calmly and without faltering. Bijou, they said, was like an older brother to them, was a good worker, and never before had caused any trouble.

In an unusual turn of events, Kushner called for a statement made by Allarie to the RCMP shortly after he awoke in the prison cell to be entered as evidence. Existence of the statement was not revealed until Kushner brought it out during cross-examination of Sergeant Reg. Alcock. When Johnston protested that the statement should not be entered, Montague asked if he did not think that justice would invite the Crown to waive its objection. "I'm putting the bundle on your doorstep," said the judge. Johnston replied that he did not wish to place any improper prejudice on the accused, and Montague ruled the statement admissible.

In the statement, taken as questions and answers, Allarie said he had no recollection of shooting the Delbridges, but admitted having an argument over wages with William Delbridge the week before the shootings. "I had an argument with Delbridge about a week ago over wages. I wanted him to pay me $100 a month and he wanted to pay me $80." Allarie said he bought two 13-ounce bottles of whisky in Portage la Prairie before returning to the dance at Poplar Point, and that he blacked out after drinking them.

Allarie expanded on the statement when called to the stand in his own defence. He said he had first gone to the beer parlour in Portage la Prairie and had been drinking with a truck driver who gave him a lift before buying the two bottles of whisky. He drank from them before taking the bus back to Poplar Point. "I don't remember how I got to the hall. I don't remember dancing, and another thing I don't remember the music." He had a vague recollection of talking with William Delbridge outside the hall and having a drink with him. After that he did not remember anything until he woke in the jail cell. Twenty-five minutes of cross-examination did not bring any change in the story.

Called as a defence witness, Dr. Gilbert Adamson, a psychiatrist, said that Allarie was a simple-minded man who he believed to be quite guileless. "I believe what he said during our interview when he said he could remember or could not remember." Answering a hypothetical question from Kushner about a man going to sleep after committing a crime of violence, Dr. Adamson said he would conclude that such a man was grossly intoxicated.

Basing his summary to the jury on the defence that Allarie was too drunk to be capable of forming an intent, Kushner called for a manslaughter verdict. "The Crown will say that it is easy to say 'I don't remember,' but this is not an ordinary case of I don't remember." He asked the jury to look for a motive; "There was none."

Johnston countered: "I suggest that he not only had the ability to form an intent, but that he had formed an intent when he went out of the way to get that rifle on the way home. He had every intention of getting that rifle when he took it without permission, and had intent when he loaded it on the way home. He took the intent all the way home with him. I'm not asking you to conjecture anything. I'm asking you to take the plain physical facts."

The jury had been retired for almost four hours when they asked for further instruction from the judge. They asked Montague to repeat and amplify his remarks on homicide while under the influence of liquor. Five minutes after Montague had done so, they returned with a verdict of guilty of murder. There was no recommendation for mercy.

Allarie took the verdict and sentence calmly. Montague sentenced him to be hanged May 2, 1950, at 12:15 a.m., or as soon thereafter as could be conveniently arranged.

With feelings running high against Allarie in Poplar Point and the surrounding community, there was little hope of an appeal for clemency being launched. The trial judge's report to the Remission Service was brief and factual. It concluded: "A perusal of the evidence will, I am convinced, establish that I left the decision on the real issue entirely to the jury. I have no personal views to communicate." Kushner could only report to the Remission Service that "the case made neither head nor tail; there was no sense to it, and there was no motive established."

A report by an RCMP constable, forwarded to the deputy minister of justice by the commissioner of the force, had no compunction about outlining a mass of rumour and speculation gathered in the Poplar Point area. None of it could have been admitted as evidence at a trial. The constable's report concluded that Allarie's intelligence was "of the lower grade," and that his morals were "of the same calibre." It described Allarie as having boasted of his conquests of women, and said that on at least one occasion he had made homosexual advances to a young man in the area. The report also purported to have found evidence of other "peculiarities," from the fact that Allarie had been found alone in a barn one morning, where he said he had gone to sleep off a night of drinking. "In view of the facts that have since come to light…and the fact that he could be somewhat of a pervert if he gets worked up, we might assume he was in the barn for the purpose of relieving his feelings with some of the animals in there."

While saying that one could only engage in conjecture regarding Allarie's motives for the shootings, the constable's report said a plausible motive was that he had become infatuated with young Joan Delbridge and, realizing that her parents would disapprove, resolved to kill the whole family and then himself.

The question arises as to why such unproven, inflammatory material should be given a place in a document bearing on the life or death of a convicted person?

The memorandum forwarded to the solicitor-general by the deputy minister of justice presented a strong case against commutation: "It would appear a dangerous precedent indeed when considering commutation, to treat as proper ground for clemency the fact that the Crown had been unable to definitely establish motive."

The solicitor-general's report was against commutation, and

the cabinet agreed. Alone, unwanted and despised, Camille Allarie had every reason to be sobbing as he went to his death.

As I sat writing my story of his and Lusanko's deaths in the *Free Press* office in the middle of the night, the night editor, Steve Wilson, approached my desk. "My God," he said, "You're drunk." I looked up from the typewriter: "How the hell do you think I could do this if I was sober?"

Chapter Ten

M'Naghten Revisited

> I was perfectly satisfied throughout that Stoney was sane
> at the time of the murder and sane at the time of his trial;
> that he thoroughly understood what was going on and
> that he knew he was guilty.
>
> —Chief Justice E.K. Williams,
> Report to the Minister of Justice

If the learned Chief Justice of the Court of King's Bench, backed by the opinion of the provincial psychiatrist, Dr. T.A. Pincock, was convinced that Walter Stoney's actions were "a pretence" aimed at gaining an acquittal on grounds of insanity, he should have been at the execution. If Stoney wasn't crazy, then he was a superb actor. To this day I cannot believe that a sane man, no matter how much he welcomed death, could enter that grisly chamber at Headingley Jail with a broad smile on his face.

Often surly and brooding during his court appearances, Stoney walked into the place of death on January 17, 1951, unsupported by the accompanying guards. Glancing around at the witnesses and smiling happily, he walked steadily to the trapdoor under the scaffold in complete silence. He was still smiling when the hangman, Camille, wearing his trademark black beret, slipped the black silk hood over his head. Twenty-five seconds after he entered the chamber at 1:04 a.m., Stoney dropped through the floor to his death.

The trial and death of Walter Stoney, an itinerant cook with a grade three education, was a classic illustration of the futility of pleading insanity as long as the M'Naghten Rules are the legal yardstick of impaired mental condition. Like M'Naghten, Stoney was suffering from a "specific delusion" that someone was trying to take his life. In this case he believed that his victim, a woman with whom he was living from time to time, was trying to poison him. Acting on that delusion, he stabbed her to death with an ice pick. He then attempted suicide by throwing himself in front of a train.

Yet, in the eyes of the judge, the provincial psychiatrist, and a jury of his peers, he was "legally sane." After passage of the years; let the reader decide.

In March 1950, 38-year-old Walter Stoney was carrying on an affair with Mrs. Martha Perrault. A dowdy, 30-year-old widow with six children, she was living in emergency welfare quarters at the former No. 3 RCAF Wireless School in suburban Tuxedo. One year previous, her husband had committed suicide by hanging himself in their home on Flora Place in north Winnipeg. It was an event that obviously played on Stoney's unstable mind. A neighbour at the emergency shelter in Tuxedo on one occasion heard him tell Mrs. Perrault: "You are not going to pull the same trick on me you did on the other guy. I'll kill you first." Mrs. Perrault snapped back; "You haven't the nerve."

On Sunday, March 11, 1950, Stoney got the nerve.

The previous evening, Mrs. Perrault left her quarters in Tuxedo with Stoney, leaving three of her children in the care of their eight-year-old brother, Albert. Two other children lived with their grandparents on a farm outside Winnipeg. She and Stoney went to his living quarters, a shabby room he had rented for the previous three months in the National Hotel, fronting onto Winnipeg's tough Main Street strip. They took a bottle of whisky with them.

At 8:35 Sunday morning, engineer Donald F. McDonald was backing up a yard engine in the CPR King Street yards a few blocks from the National Hotel, when he saw a man writhing on the ground beside a nearby track. An east-bound train had passed by some three minutes earlier. It was Stoney, his right arm mangled and bloody, trying to get up. McDonald's fireman, Floyd Lovelace, climbed down from the cab of the engine and covered Stoney with his coat. Before the ambulance and police arrived, the injured man had lapsed into unconsciousness. He would spend the greater part of that day on an operating table in Winnipeg General Hospital as surgeons fought to save his life.

Unable to question Stoney, police examined identification papers in his wallet and went to Room 45 at the National Hotel. When the room clerk, Max Melnik, let them into the room, a strong smell of alcohol hung in the fetid air. An empty whisky bottle and two glasses stood on a table near the bed. On the floor beside the bed was a pool of blood and the walls of the room were spattered with gore. Under the bed was the body of Mrs. Perrault, her clothing pierced by eighteen stab wounds and saturated with blood. Her black cloth coat had been shoved in on top of her along with a heap of blood-soaked rags. They apparently had been used in a futile attempt to clean the blood from the floor and walls. Inside a drawer, wiped clean, detectives found the murder weapon. It was an ice pick 15 inches long.

On the dresser was a note in Stoney's laboured handwriting: "Mrs. Perrault and Stoney have been leave [sic] together for last four months. For first two months O.K. Then Mrs. Perrault started to give me poison. I have to kill her and myself because my heart is weak since she give me something in food."

Three days later, as Stoney slipped in and out of consciousness, two detectives were sent to interview him when his condition appeared to worsen. When Detective Sergeant Alex Price asked Stoney what had happened in his room, Stoney replied: "She was going to kill me and took the ice pick and I knocked the pick… She grabbed the pick and scratched my hand. I knocked it down, picked it up and hit her with it. I went to CPR to take train and was going to go under wheels. I went insane. I had the same thing in Port Arthur in 1934."

It was not until almost two months after the slaying that Stoney could be charged with murder on his release from the hospital on May 4. At the preliminary hearing before Magistrate Maris Garton on July 11, Stoney appeared without counsel. As the evidence unfolded, he appeared confused and distraught. Halfway through the first day of evidence, Stoney rose and said he could not continue. "I have nobody to represent me, and I do not understand half of what is being said."

When a handwriting expert was called to the stand the next day, Stoney again declared that he did not know what was going on and said he could not continue. Magistrate Garton was unsympathetic: "You have had lots of time to obtain counsel. You could have done so overnight." He then assured Stoney that he would be represented by a lawyer at his trial.

On July 13, after three days of hearing, Stoney was committed for trial and bound over to the Fall Assizes.

Over the next three-and-a-half months awaiting his trial, Stoney proved a stubborn and difficult prisoner refusing on occasion to shave or have his hair cut. His guards noted that he slept fitfully, but that he ate well. When he appeared at the arraignment for the Fall Assizes on October 17, 1950, he still did not have counsel.

Escorted to the dock by guards, Stoney was asked to stand while the charge of murdering Mrs. Perrault was read to him. Emotionless, he turned to look at Mr. Justice J.J. Kelly and declared: "I am guilty." Noting that he was not represented by counsel, the judge instructed the court clerk to enter a plea of not guilty, and informed Stoney that he was appointing Samuel Freedman as his counsel. The trial date was set for October 30, with Chief Justice Williams presiding.

Turning to Stoney, Kelly asked: "Do you understand that?"

"I am guilty my lord."

"I cannot accept your plea. Your counsel will instruct you on your rights. The prisoner will be removed from the box and the press will not report that a guilty plea was entered."

Following the judge's instruction, the press refrained from reporting Stoney's insistence on his guilt pending the outcome of his trial. There was a repeat of the performance when Stoney's trial opened on October 30. Again he insisted on pleading guilty, and again the press was instructed to refrain from reporting his confession of guilt. However, the judicial restriction against revealing the guilty plea was lifted on the third day of the trial. At the morning session Stoney tried to plead guilty again, this time in front of the jury. There was no longer any danger of jeopardizing a fair trial by reporting his insistence of guilt.

Left with little choice as the damning evidence built up against his client, Freedman called Stoney to the stand to testify in his own defence. His face pale and grim, Stoney took the stand. Freedman began his questions: "You were in a train accident. Do you remember?"

Turning to the judge and then the jury, Stoney mumbled: "My lord and gentlemen of the jury. I am pretty sick, and I decided to plead guilty."

Again asked if he remembered the train accident, Stoney replied: "Yes, but my lord, I mean that I want to plead guilty."

"Stoney, do you remember being in a train accident?"

"I don't want to go through with it. I can't go through with it. I can't go through with the questions. I am very sick."

Patiently persisting in his questioning, Freedman managed to extract a few mumbled replies from his confused client. Finally, an interpreter was called and sworn. At the first question in Ukrainian, Stoney made a helpless gesture with his hands and began to speak rapidly in his native language: "I'm too sick. I cannot go through with it."

Turning to the chief justice, Freedman said he intended to continue his questioning. "I take the view this is one circumstance

of many the gentlemen of the jury are entitled to consider."
However, under further questioning, Stoney continued to reply
that he was too sick to answer: "Maybe this afternoon I will feel
better."

"Were you at No. 3 Wireless School with Mrs. Perrault?"

"At the present time my lord I cannot give any answer."

After about 15 minutes of muttered and sometimes unintel-
ligible answers, Freedman was granted an adjournment to the
afternoon sitting.

When court reopened at 2 p.m., Dr. J.J. Bourgouin was called
as a defence witness. He knew Stoney as a patient, and on January
23, Stoney brought a specimen of his urine to his office and asked
to have it examined for poison. "He said he believed he was being
poisoned by his common-law wife. He said he had been with her
for two or three months. I formed the opinion that he was not
himself, though not insane. I advised him to take any food he
suspected of being poisoned to the provincial laboratory for
analysis."

In a final attempt to extract some intelligible replies from
Stoney, Freedman again called him to the stand.

Freedman began: "Do you think I am against you Stoney?"

In a scarcely audible voice, Stoney looked at the judge: "I
don't know whether you for or against me."

"Didn't I bring you tobacco?"

Before Stoney could reply, Williams intervened: "I appreciate your position Mr. Freedman, but he is addressing me and I
would like him to finish."

"I pleaded guilty."

The chief justice patiently explained: "This is a murder
charge. If you are found guilty, the penalty is death by hanging.
You say you want to plead guilty. One of the reasons the court is
here is to make sure no man is convicted of a crime he did not
commit. That's why we didn't want you to plead guilty. Mr.
Freedman is doing the very best he can for you. Interpreter, tell

him if he is guilty he will have to be hanged."

His hands clasped in front of him, Stoney replied through the interpreter: "I said to my counsel this morning my lord, I'm guilty and that's all there is to it."

"For the last time Stoney, I am going to ask you to answer Mr. Freedman's questions. He's doing it for your own good."

Freedman tried again: "Do you remember what happened in your room on March 11?"

"I told you this morning; I plead guilty."

"Do you remember what happened March 11?"

"I plead guilty," Stoney replied through the interpreter.

Williams again intervened: "You have fully discharged your duty Mr. Freedman. Stoney, you will have to go back to the dock now."

As Stoney was escorted back to the prisoner's dock, Freedman asked that the jury be retired. In their absence he said there was reason to doubt Stoney's fitness to stand trial. He moved that the accused's sanity be made an issue for decision by the court under Section 197 of the Criminal Code.

Saying he was neither opposing or consenting to the test of Stoney's sanity, Crown counsel Charles Tupper said he would leave the issue to the court.

Rejecting the motion, Williams ruled there was nothing before him to permit him to exercise his discretion regarding Stoney's fitness or otherwise. The jury was recalled. The chief justice was vacillating. His later report clearly showed that he had already made up his mind that Stoney was fit to stand trial and was cunningly trying to deceive the court.

Called by the Crown as a rebuttal to the defence witnesses, Dr. Pincock, the provincial psychiatrist, said he had examined Stoney several times between March and October of 1950. On some occasions, Stoney had been co-operative and had appeared to understand English well. There had been no difficulty in taking his history. "He convinced me he was fit to stand trial, to instruct his counsel and to follow proceedings." However, there were other interviews when Stoney was rebellious and resistant, and had behaved much as he had done while on the witness stand in court. "There were times when I could question him, and other times when I could not."

But, said Dr. Pincock, he had formed the opinion that Stoney was legally sane, aware of the consequences of his acts, and aware of the difference between right and wrong at the time of the incident of which he was accused.

He was expressing a classic definition of the infamous M'Naghten Rules. The dead hands of 14 judges of the High Court of England had reached over a century to fasten on the throat of Walter Stoney.

"What about his state today? Are you of the opinion Stoney's performance in the box was an act?" asked Freedman.

"I would not say his performance was an escape. It appears to be a conscious or unconscious attempt to avoid a painful situation or conversation. I cannot reconcile his conduct today with the way he conducted himself at the interviews."

Faced with the difficult task of trying to save a man in spite of himself; Freedman made an eloquent plea for a manslaughter verdict. Stoney's sanity or insanity was the first question to be considered. The second was whether or not Stoney was so drunk he could not, and did not, know what he was doing and was incapable of forming an intent. The third point was whether or not Stoney's drunken state, coupled with provocation, properly made his offence manslaughter.

Tupper countered by contending that the death room had been cleaned up, and the bed turned and re-made to hide bloodstains while the body was hidden under it. "Is this the act of a crazed or drunken man, or the act of a man who wants to cover up his deed to give him time to escape from town?"

Chief Justice Williams ended his charge to the jury at 11:37 a.m. on the fourth day of the trial. At seven minutes past noon, the jury returned with their verdict. They had rejected the insanity plea. Stoney was guilty of murder. "I concur entirely in the verdict," said Williams.

Stoney showed absolutely no emotion as the verdict was announced. Asked if he had anything to say before sentence was passed, he replied: "Yes, my belongings I want sent down east, and the ones that were in my room I want to go to my cousin in Winnipeg."

For the fourth time, Chief Justice Williams placed the black cloth on his head and pronounced the death sentence. Stoney was to hang on January 17, 1951, at Headingley Jail.

Shortly before the sentence was to be carried out, there appeared to be some concern in Ottawa about the propriety of executing someone who might be mentally ill. On January 9, Dr. J.P.S. Cathcart, a psychiatrist with the Department of Veteran's Affairs in Ottawa, flew to Winnipeg. He examined Stoney in the death cell at Headingley.

He reported that the condemned man was "definitely pre-psychotic," and that he and Dr. Pincock agreed that he would gradually become insane. Noting that the prosecutor and other Crown officials had indicated they were inclined to view the exercise of clemency favourably, Cathcart suggested that in view of Stoney's violent tendencies, it would be unwise to have him released from prison for many years to come. There was every indication that the psychiatrist expected the sentence to be commuted.

In addition, the attorney-general's department in Manitoba informed the deputy minister of justice in Ottawa that, "apart altogether from the problem of insanity, none of the officials connected with the case will quarrel with commutation. This takes into account a certain degree of intoxication, a lack of planning and premeditation, and the apparent attempt to commit suicide…"

Thus, the memorandum from the deputy minister of justice

that went forward to Justice Minister Stuart Garson on January 13, 1951, concluded: "In the circumstances, and in keeping with constant practice in capital cases in which arises the question of mentality impaired to such an advanced degree, the undersigned is of the opinion the death sentence may well be commuted to life imprisonment."

One can only conjecture why, in the face of that report and recommendation, Garson made a report to cabinet that was against commutation. The deputy minister, the medical personnel consulted and the provincial justice officials all favoured the exercise of clemency by commutation of the death sentence. The record is silent on what passed in the cabinet room. But, before being appointed as federal minister of justice in 1948, Garson had been premier of Manitoba when Williams was appointed chief justice of the Manitoba Court of King's Bench. Garson and Williams had been friends as members of the Manitoba bar, and the trial judge's report was the only one unfavourable to commutation.

Said Williams: "I had no doubt in my mind that the accused was not only quite able to stand his trial, but was seeking to create an impression that he was not… I was perfectly satisfied throughout that Stoney was sane at the time of the murder and sane at the time of the trial; that he thoroughly understood what was going on and that he knew he was guilty."

That damning indictment obviously offset other concerns, including a last minute memorandum to Garson from Dr. Cathcart noting that the issue of whether Stoney had been suffering from a "specific delusion" that the victim had been trying to poison him, had not been raised at the trial.

On January 17, 1951, when Stoney went happily to his death, he was to have been accompanied by Henry Malanik, a burly 48-year-old plumber convicted of the shotgun slaying of a Winnipeg detective. But, Malanik had been granted a stay of execution awaiting a decision on an appeal to the Manitoba Court of

Appeal.

Over a year later following a second trial, Malanik's blood would spatter the walls of the death chamber at Headingley. E.K. Williams had pronounced his fifth death sentence on the last man to hang in Manitoba.

Chapter Eleven

Homebrew and Bad Blood

Sunday, July 16, 1950. I was enjoying a leisurely morning. I had put on my uniform in preparation to leaving for the airport to take part in the weekend activities of the City of Winnipeg, 402 RCAF Auxiliary Squadron, when the phone rang. It was the city editor. Gordon Sinclair, our police reporter, would be around in a few minutes to pick me up. There had been a late Saturday night shoot-out; a policeman was dead, and Gord and I were to go to the scene and dig up everything we could.

Cursing my bad luck, I grudgingly discarded my uniform for my street clothes. There was no overtime pay at the *Winnipeg Free Press* for working on a Sunday, and I was about to lose a day's pay as a reserve Flight Lieutenant.

Some of the irritation faded at the shooting scene. We had a dramatic story on our hands. It began with the knifing of one man by his boyhood friend in an argument over the affections of the stabbing victim's wife. It culminated with a police ambulance carrying three other wounded men to hospital. One of them, Detective Sergeant James "Ted" Sims, died shortly afterwards as the result of a gaping wound in his abdomen caused by a shotgun blast at close range.

The scene of the mayhem was a small two-storey house at 19 Argyle Street in the Point Douglas area of Winnipeg, just off North Main Street. It was an area of lower class working homes interspersed with industrial and commercial sites along the CPR mainline yards. The house still stands just to the right of where the double-humped Disraeli Freeway begins its first rise to clear the rail yards, then rises again to cross the Red River.

A barrage of gunfire had erupted in the small home about midnight Saturday, and we spent a busy day interviewing neighbours, sketching the ground plan of the house, and photographing bullet-scarred walls. We pieced together the major points for a story on the front page the next day. The details were fleshed out during the trial.

The circumstances that led to Henry Malanik being charged with murder began some time before the Saturday night tragedy. A plumber, Malanik came to Canada as a child in 1912. He never progressed beyond grade four. At the age of 17, he was sentenced to a year in jail on seven charges of breaking and entering. He had no further trouble with the law until 1950. His boyhood friend, Adolph Kafka, was the best man at his marriage in 1929. When Malanik's wife left him in 1948, he moved in with Kafka and his wife Olga as a boarder at 457 Henry Avenue, a short distance from 19 Argyle Street.

Adolph Kafka's work kept him out of town for extended periods, and during his absence his friend Malanik and Olga Kafka began an affair. Kafka learned of the affair. Ejected from the house, Malanik went to live in a room at 671 Main Street, one of the shabby buildings facing onto Winnipeg's skid-row. Malanik continued to see Olga after she and her husband moved into her parent's home at 19 Argyle. On April 18, 1950, the two former friends tangled again over Olga's affections. Firearms were discharged, and police called to the Argyle Street home seized a twelve-gauge shotgun from Malanik and two 22 calibre rifles and a pistol from Adolph Kafka.

Charged with discharging firearms, both men were fined $50 and warned to avoid each other. Tragically, the weapons were returned to the combatants in early July.

On Saturday, July 15, Malanik got up at 10 a.m. in the Main Street room he shared with a friend, Bill Krystik. A member of

Krystik's family was to be married that day, but Malanik was reluctant to attend the wedding as his estranged wife was expected to be there. However, after going out for breakfast, Malanik returned and had several drinks of whisky before leaving for the wedding. After meeting and shaking hands with his wife, he went downstairs at the Winnipeg Rumanian Association Hall where the reception was held.

The reception was an uninhibited affair with homebrew flowing freely. Bill Krystik, who was the bartender, said Malanik was drinking the fiery fluid a half tumbler-full at a time. Obviously, he was one of the more boisterous of the celebrants. Drunks were seldom ejected from such affairs, but Malanik managed it. Shortly before 11 p.m., Malanik outstayed his welcome by cursing and swearing at the members of the orchestra when they refused to play during the intermission, and for generally making himself obnoxious.

Detective Sergeant Ted Sims checked in early that night for his midnight to 8 a.m. tour of duty. As he walked into the detective headquarters at the Rupert Avenue police station at 11:45 p.m. a call came in. A cruiser car constable reported that a stabbing had taken place. Sims turned to two young acting detectives, William Anderson and John Peachell: "There's trouble again over at 19 Argyle. You fellows better take this call." Then, although his shift had not yet begun, he decided to go with them. When he left to travel the five short blocks to Argyle Street, Sims' service revolver was left behind, locked in his desk.

Olga Kafka's parents, Mr. and Mrs. William Wasylanchuk, occupied the first floor at 19 Argyle while Olga and her husband lived on the second floor. Her sister-in-law occupied a bedroom in the basement. Shortly after 11 a.m., Malanik arrived asking to see Olga. William Wasylanchuk met him, and they went into the yard to talk. On leave from his job at Pine Falls in rural Manitoba, Adolph Kafka heard Malanik and vowed to go down and have it out with his former friend once and for all.

Olga tried, but failed to restrain her husband. He went downstairs, and a few minutes later returned bleeding from knife wounds. Malanik had stabbed him three times with an army dagger. Olga phoned police, then went outside and told Malanik that he was drunk and should go home. Adolph Kafka was taken to the hospital. His wounds were dressed and he was allowed to return home.

Meanwhile, Sims, Anderson and Peachell arrived to find both Malanik and Kafka gone. While they were questioning Olga Kafka in the kitchen, a drunken, enraged Malanik had gone back to his Main Street Room. He was now returning to the stabbing scene by a circuitous route.

Victor McLean, a commissionaire employed as a night guard at the Empire Sash and Door Lumber Yard, three doors south of the Wasylanchuk home, was about to go on duty. Seeing a shadowy figure approaching, he stopped at the corner of Argyle Street and Henry Avenue. The figure emerged from the shadows and he recognized Malanik who he had seen visiting 19 Argyle on previous occasions. Malanik appeared to be carrying a club beside his leg. Approaching the commissionaire, Malanik brought the object up and levelled it at McLean's chest. It was the twelve-gauge Browning over-under shotgun that police had returned to Malanik a short time earlier. "Make one move and I'll blast you," threatened Malanik. McLean first tried to placate the drunken man. But, Malanik kept repeating his threat and became more agitated. McLean, an army veteran, decided that discretion was truly the better part of valour and stood aside. As he went to phone police, Malanik lurched toward 19 Argyle.

Peachell was seated with Olga Kafka in a breakfast nook in the kitchen, taking notes on the stabbing. Sims stood leaning in the doorway between the kitchen and the small downstairs living room. Anderson went outside with a flashlight to look around and had just returned to the kitchen by the back door. Suddenly, there was the sound of footsteps in the front hall. Sims turned and walked half-way into the living room. Anderson followed and stood by one side of the door.

Pandemonium followed. Malanik entered from the hallway with the shotgun levelled from his hip shouting; "I'm going to shoot you all." Sims raised his hands: "Don't be foolish man. Put down that gun." The roar of the shotgun bounced off the walls of the small room as the full load of No. 4 shot caught Sims in the abdomen tearing open a three-inch wound. Clasping his hands to his stomach, Sims staggered backward into the kitchen. He collapsed onto the floor calling for the other detectives to help him.

In the basement bedroom, Olga Kafka's sister-in-law screamed and shouted for Olga. Peachell jumped from the breakfast nook and pulled his revolver. Olga dived for the basement stairs and went down them. Anderson pulled his gun and jumped back into the kitchen. Peachell snapped off a shot in the general direction of Malanik in the living room, then moved to the wall and carefully looked around the kitchen doorway. Malanik was standing in the middle of the living room with the shotgun still levelled. Peachell pulled back his head just as the shotgun roared again. Splinters flew from the door jamb near where his head had been.

After a moment, Peachell jumped across the open doorway to get to a telephone in the far corner of the kitchen. Meanwhile, Anderson backed out of the kitchen into an adjoining bedroom where William Wasylanchuk was giving some pills to his wife who was in bed. Anderson jumped out through the window. Intending to cut off Malanik's escape, he passed by the south side of the house and looked in through the living room window. Malanik had backed to the hallway to reload, and was standing in the doorway. Anderson broke the window with his revolver, and pumped off three quick shots at the shadowy figure. He then ran around to the front door and took another shot at what he thought was Malanik. Returning to the side window, Anderson looked in but could not see anyone. Turning back to the front door, he heard a series of shots inside the house. Malanik had reloaded the shotgun and walked into the kitchen.

Peachell was at the telephone desperately trying to dial for help with his left hand while holding his revolver pointed at the kitchen door with his right hand. Malanik emerged through the door with the shotgun just under his armpit and pointed it in the direction of the frantic detective. Peachell opened fire, emptying the remaining five shots from his 38 calibre Smith and Wesson at Malanik. Reaching the middle of the kitchen, Malanik brought the shotgun higher, pointed it directly at Peachell's chest from a distance of a few feet and pulled the trigger. There was a clicking sound as the shotgun jerked upward. Then Malanik collapsed onto the kitchen floor at Peachell's feet.

Stepping aside, Peachell ran into the living room and out the front door. There he joined Anderson and they crouched behind some bushes. Leaving Peachell to watch the front door, Anderson headed for the cruiser car parked in the street intending to radio for an ambulance and further help. He had just reached the rear of the cruiser when a shot rang out. Anderson fell, wounded in the neck. A rookie constable, responding to the call put in by commissionaire McLean, had fired at Anderson thinking he was Malanik fleeing the scene.

Inside the house, Malanik staggered to his feet still carrying the shotgun and stumbled into the bedroom off the kitchen. Mrs. Wasylanchuk was in bed and her husband was standing at the side of the room. Malanik, who had been hit three times and had bullet wounds to his left hand, shoulder and hip, sat down on the bed. Speaking rapidly in Ukrainian, Wasylanchuk sat down beside Malanik. Taking the shotgun from his now limp hands, the older man threw it against the wall behind the bed where it dropped to the floor with a thud.

Shocked into sensibility by his wounds, Malanik rose, walked back into the kitchen and dropped to the floor beside the mortally wounded Sims. Throwing his arm around Sims' shoulder, Malanik began to cry. He was still lying there when Peachell returned to the kitchen, accompanied by McLean whose call had brought an ambulance to the scene. As they entered they could hear Malanik repeating: "Don't die Ted. I didn't mean to shoot you Ted. Don't die. I didn't mean to shoot you."

Within minutes, all three wounded men were in the police ambulance racing to Winnipeg General Hospital. Ironically, Malanik who had walked through a fusillade of ten bullets fired at distances of ten feet or less, was the least seriously wounded of the three. Anderson would recover from his neck wound to testify at Malanik's trial, but Sims died at 6:30 a.m. following emergency surgery.

Peachell, who fired six shots at Malanik from a distance of a few feet, was lucky to be alive. When Malanik's shotgun was recovered from behind the Wasylanchuk's bed, one expended and one live shell were found in the chambers. On the end of the cap of the live shell there was a slight indentation. The firing pin had struck the cap, but with insufficient force to explode the charge of heavy shot. It was the click that Peachell heard before Malanik fell at his feet in the kitchen.

The expended shell in the other barrel also gave evidence of a near miss for Anderson when he broke the window and fired from outside the house at Malanik in the hall doorway. In the sill of the window were shotgun pellets, and the wadding from the shell was imbedded in the window drape.

While the evidence given by Anderson and Peachell in court was unclear as to how many shots Malanik fired, several clues uncovered after the wild shooting melée showed the probable sequence of events. There were three shotgun waddings in the living room, showing the shotgun had been fired three times. Four splinters of wood were found lying beside the stairs in the front hallway. They fitted into a jagged gash on the left side of the stock of Malanik's shotgun just above the trigger guard. Unlike most double-barrel shotguns which have two triggers, one for each barrel, the Browning over-under has a single trigger. When the first barrel is fired, it throws a small tumbler inside the gun that shifts over and the second barrel can then be fired. A bullet had struck the stock and knocked out the tumbler. Without it, the second barrel could not be fired. That saved Peachell's life.

The location of the wood splinters and the pellets imbedded in the window frame showed that, after shooting Sims and firing the second barrel at Peachell when he looked round the door, Malanik backed to the hall. He had just reloaded both barrels when one of the bullets fired through the window by Anderson, struck the shotgun, and probably caused the wound to Malanik's left hand. Malanik fired at Anderson, hitting the window frame, and then lurched toward the kitchen. The wonder is that the force of the hit on the heavy shotgun did not knock it out of Malanik's hands.

One thing is certain: it was not a day that would rate high in the annals of the Winnipeg police force. A volley of revolver fire at point-blank range had almost missed the berserk gunman. At one point Malanik, having fired both barrels, was holding an empty gun that could have been wrested from him. Instead, one detective went out the bedroom window leaving an elderly couple unprotected in the bedroom. The other went to the telephone, allowing Malanik time to reload. Then, when Malanik collapsed in the kitchen, Peachell inexplicably ran outside instead of reaching down and picking up the shotgun. It was left to the elderly man in the bedroom to take the shotgun from Malanik and throw it behind the bed while the two detectives crouched in the shrubbery in the front yard. To cap it all off, another policeman arrived on the scene, and without warning, critically wounded a fellow officer. (The rookie who fired the shot was not authorized to carry a weapon. He was discharged from the force shortly after, following an internal investigation.)

In the ambulance on the way to the hospital, Malanik was

filled with remorse. Constable George Curle recorded the wounded man's ramblings in his notebook: "I'm sorry I did it. I had a few drinks. He did his duty that man did. I want to die now. There is a dead man who should not die."

At the hospital while waiting on a stretcher as doctors attended to the more seriously wounded police officers, Malanik muttered replies to police questioning.

"Where were you going tonight?"

"I don't know."

"Where did the shooting take place?"

"I don't know."

"What were you carrying the shotgun shells in your pocket for?"

"Kiss my ass will you."

The mood changed and the litany of regrets began again: "I am sorry I shot an innocent man. He started to interfere in my affairs. I told him to get out of the way, but he wouldn't. I never would have shot him if had not alcohol in me. Maybe if I hadn't drunk homebrew, maybe I never done what I did. I don't want that man to die. He shot first and then I pulled the trigger. I don't give a shit what happens to me. I know it's going to be the rope. That's all the statements I have sir."

The death of Sergeant Sims sparked an outcry against the inadequate provisions for the families of police officers killed in the line of duty. The Winnipeg Chamber of Commerce made representations to the city council to establish an insurance fund, or some other method for the financial protection of police officers or firemen. Simultaneously, the Chamber launched an appeal for contributions to a fund to smooth the path of Sims' widow and three children. Public contributions to the fund were $8,051.13. Invested in an annuity, it provided the family of the slain officer with $76.75 a month over the following ten years. That parsimonious sum made even our low reporters' salaries look good.

Fully recovered from his wounds, Malanik went on trial for the first time on October 17, 1950, in a courtroom presided over by Mr. Justice J.J. Kelly. A young lawyer, J.L. Crawford, who once made the news pages as a look-alike for Babe Ruth, conducted the defence. He had little to fall back on, other than to fight for a manslaughter verdict. Malanik, he said, was too drunk to have been capable of forming an intent. "The man was sodden right back through his mind; he couldn't intend to do anything."

Testifying in his own defence, Malanik told the jury that he could not remember anything after having a number of tumblers of homebrew at the wedding party. "The next thing I was laying down on a floor and there was lots of blood. I noticed a policeman. Then there were two blows on my chest and someone said, 'you've killed two policemen.' The next thing I remember after that was being strapped to a bed when I came to."

Several witnesses from the wedding reception testified that Malanik had been drinking heavily and had been asked to leave the party about 11 p.m. when he used abusive language and began to fight with members of the orchestra.

The final defence witness was Dr. Gilbert Adamson, a psychiatrist. He said that a person suffering from amnesia caused by excessive intoxication might carry out purposeful acts, but their normal planning and carrying out of such acts and their persistence to carry it out might be impaired. Normally, such an act would be impulsive and not planned, he said, and a degree of gross intoxication would be necessary to reach such a condition.

Crown Counsel W.J. Johnston blasted the defence theory in a 35-minute address to the jury. Malanik had formed an intent, he said. "This was no purposeless action. He didn't go and get a gun and fire aimlessly and wildly around him. He proceeded with a purpose... Only after his gun had been damaged and Malanik himself wounded and no longer able to carry out his intent, did he have remorse."

The jury agreed. It took them only 40 minutes to return a

verdict of guilty of murder. Mr. Justice Kelly placed the black cloth on his head and sentenced Malanik to be hanged on January 17, 1951. He did so with misgivings, as his report to the higher court showed after Crawford appealed the murder conviction.

The trial judge wrote: "I must say that had I been sitting as judge without a jury in a similar case, I would have had a doubt as to whether or not the accused was capable of knowing what he was doing, or of knowing right from wrong. In my opinion, the accused was very drunk. I concluded that he went 'berserk' at 19 Argyle Street, otherwise I cannot understand why he would shoot at everyone who came in sight; first Sims, then Peachell when he put his head around the kitchen door and again Peachell in the kitchen when the gun jammed. He had no grievance against those police officers, in fact, it does not appear that he knew either Anderson or Peachell."

On February 2, the Manitoba Court of Appeal reserved decision on Malanik's appeal after earlier granting a stay of execution to March 9. Three days before that date, Malanik's conviction was quashed and a new trial ordered in one of the most divided decisions handed down by the five-man court.

Chief Justice McPherson and Mr. Justice Adamson said they would reduce the conviction to manslaughter and commute the death penalty to life imprisonment. Noting Kelly's doubts whether Malanik knew right from wrong, they said it was not only the right of the trial judge, but his duty to express such opinions to the jury. In view of the evidence of drunkenness, no reasonable jury, properly instructed, could find Malanik guilty of murder, said Adamson.

Mr. Justice Dysart agreed that the question of intent was not fully or accurately put to the jury, but said he would rule for a new trial. Mr. Justice Montague said; "With great reluctance, I concur with my brother Adamson, but with the exception that I would grant a new trial rather than reduce the conviction to manslaughter."

The odd-man-out, Mr. Justice Coyne, said he felt the trial judge's charge to the jury had been "eminently fair, true and accurate." He would deny the appeal and let the murder conviction stand. However, the majority of the court having ruled for setting aside the conviction, he would vote for a new trial.

Malanik went on trial before a second jury in late May 1951, with Chief Justice Williams presiding. With the ruling of the appeal court in mind, Williams' charge to the jury was carefully framed and took 90 minutes to complete. This time there appeared to be doubts in the minds of the jurors. They took almost ten hours to reach a verdict. Halfway through their deliberations, they asked for further instruction on the law concerning drunkenness and the ability to form an intent.

The final decision came at 9:55 p.m., five minutes before the jury was to be locked up for the night. Malanik was again found guilty of murder. Asked if he had anything to say before sentence was passed, he replied: "Your lordship, only this have I to say— I am innocent."

For the fifth and last time, Chief Justice Williams placed the black silk cloth on his head and pronounced the death sentence. Malanik was to be hanged at Headingley Jail on August 21, 1951. Turning to the jury, Williams thanked them for the care and consideration they had given the case and completely agreed with their verdict.

His sincerity in that concurrence was borne out later by his report to the minister of justice in Ottawa:

"Unlike Mr. Justice Kelly who presided at the first trial, I had no doubt that the accused knew exactly what he was doing; was capable of forming an intent; did form the intent, and fully appreciated the consequence of his acts. In my opinion, the evidence could lead to one conclusion, namely that while he was intoxicated he was not so intoxicated as to be entitled to a verdict of manslaughter or acquittal on the ground of temporary drunkenness amounting to insanity."

Crawford again launched an appeal. This time there was only one dissent on the five-man appeal court. Mr. Justice Coyne read the majority decision that there was indisputably sufficient evidence for the jury to convict Malanik of murder. "There was no miscarriage of justice, and I entirely agree with the learned trial judge's charge which was right and proper. There was no substantial wrong done to Malanik," said Coyne.

Chief Justice McPherson concurred along with Justices Dysart and Montague. Mr. Justice Adamson stuck to his guns and dissented. He would again have reduced the conviction to manslaughter. He was sorry to have to disagree with his fellow judges; "but I feel very strongly the defence was not fairly and fully put to the jury… The charge of the trial judge belittled the defence witnesses and the question of intoxication, and failed to point out many important aspects of the evidence."

Adamson's dissent allowed Crawford to carry an appeal to the Supreme Court in Ottawa. On May 12 that court held that it could find no flaw in the trial judge's charge to the jury and the appeal was unanimously dismissed.

Malanik's final hope disappeared on June 13. The federal cabinet declined to interfere with the sentence of the court. The summary prepared by justice department officials noted there was no recommendation for mercy from the jury, and cited Chief Justice Williams' report. The summary was unfavourable to commutation:

"As to leniency, or granting of any exercise of the Royal Prerogative, there is no recommendation by the jury or by the trial judge. The jury apparently did not give full credence to the credibility of the statements adduced at trial by certain witnesses for the defence, nor to the statements of the accused regarding his actions and degree of intoxication… There exists no ground for purely sympathetic consideration. In the circumstances, the undersigned inclines to the view that the law may well be allowed to take its course."

I covered the trials, but thank God I was not there when some 40 witnesses, including more than a dozen city detectives and uniformed police officers, crowded into the execution chamber shortly after 2 a.m. on June 17, 1952.

Henry Malanik walked into the death chamber at 2:11 a.m. He had shaved off his thin moustache and looked much older than at his trials. He was wearing a white open-necked silk shirt and the brown trousers of the neatly tailored suit he had worn at both of his trials. On his feet were grey prison socks.

Escorted by guards and Salvation Army Major Stanley McKinley, he walked unaided to the gallows. As he approached the trap, Malanik smiled at the guards and appeared to make a gesture of thanks. As the black hood was being placed over the doomed man's head, Major McKinley closed his eyes and began the Lord's Prayer. In a firm, clear voice Malanik repeated each line in response.

He had just spoken the words "…thy will be done," when Camille, wearing his black beret and an incongruous bright-flowered Hawaiian shirt, pulled the lever and Malanik plunged through the floor.

Consternation followed the reverberating crash of the heavy doors. The heavy-set Malanik was dangling at the end of the rope with his head twisted at an awful angle. Blood was spurting from under the black hood staining the floor and walls of the pit. The heavy rope had partly decapitated him and severed his jugular vein.

At 2:13 a.m., two minutes after the trap was sprung, the prison doctor, Dr. John Roy Martin, pronounced Malanik dead. Few of the nauseated witnesses were still in the chamber when he did so.

It was the last time a man died at Headingley Jail in the most modern and "humane" execution chamber in Canada.

Epilogue

Were human judgement about guilt infallible, still a death penalty would be immoral because no man may morally play God. But such a thesis need not be considered, for it assumes the impossible. Experience teaches the fallibility of court decisions. The courts have held many an innocent man guilty. How dare any society take the chance of ordering the judicial homicide of an innocent man?

—Judge Jerome Frank,
Preface to *Reflections on Hanging*

There have been renewed calls for the reintroduction of the death penalty in Canada. The impetus has been led primarily by the Reform Party of Canada who continue to call for a national referendum on the restoration of capital punishment. However, they have not been alone. Meeting in Victoria, B.C., in September of 1995, Canada's top police officers also asked Ottawa to reinstate the death penalty. Neal Jessop, president of the Canadian Police Association, in making the call, said Canadians were outraged that Paul Bernardo, convicted of the brutal and degrading deaths of two Ontario teenagers, could possibly apply for early parole after serving only a portion of his life sentence. And, in the wake of the horrific evidence presented at the Bernardo trial, a Canada-wide poll showed 69 per cent of Canadians moderately or strongly favour a return of the death penalty.

A particularly brutal murder, or series of murders, invariably results in calls for restoration. Forgotten in this surge toward what has been termed a "violence panic" by Professor Elliot Leyton, author of several books on violent crime, are the miscarriages of justice that from time to time mar the course of our legal system. For each Paul Bernardo or Clifford Olson there have been distressing tales of wrongful conviction. Since the death penalty was abolished in Canada we have witnessed a number of cases where accused murderers have spent long years in prison only to be exonerated by the discovery of new evidence. They include the conviction of Donald Marshall in the Nova Scotia and, more recently, Guy Paul Morin in Ontario. Marshall was released after the key witness at his trial subsequently confessed to the murder and Morin was released after DNA tests proved that he did not murder his neighbour Christine Jessop.

Prior to abolishment of the noose in Canada there were others who were not so fortunate. Professor Neil Boyd, a criminologist at Simon Fraser University, researched 120 cases of murder in Canada which led to the gallows. Four or five of those cases contained very little evidence of murder. In fact, some seemed to be clear cases of self defence. In about 20 other cases, he said, the evidence clearly supported a conviction on a lesser charge.

In Britain there have been several uncontroverted cases of innocent men being hanged. Timothy Evans, executed in 1950 after he was found guilty of murdering his young daughter was subsequently cleared. It is cold comfort that he was the only man ever to receive an official posthumous pardon. In another case, a court found in 1993 that Derek Bentley, hanged in 1953 at the age of 19 for allegedly murdering a policeman, was wrongly executed. And, had the noose not been abolished in Britain, there is little doubt that the "Birmingham Six" and the "Guildford Four," groups of mainly Irish people who were framed by police and subsequently sentenced to life imprisonment for supposedly taking part in terrorist bombings, would have been executed. All this in a nation that has long been renowned for the fairness and impartiality of its judicial system.

Of the seven cases outlined in this book there is one (Deacon) where there is far more than a reasonable doubt as to his guilt. Three of the others were simple-minder illiterates or near-illiterates, and none had a high-school education. One was an obvious madman. Surely, this is the same segment of our population that would be in the shadow of the gallows if capital punishment returned. The threat of hanging was no deterrent to any of the crimes.

For those who still cling to the myth of the deterrent effect of capital punishment in the clamour for restitution of the death penalty, a look at the experience in the United States would be in order. The death penalty is in effect in 38 of the 50 states. That has had little effect on soaring crime rates. The homicide rate in the U.S.A. is almost 10 per 100,000 population each year, and is higher in many of the retentionist states than it is in the abolition-ist states. That is 10 times the rate of one per 100,000 in Great Britain and five times the rate of two per 100,000 in Canada. Two countries where the death penalty no longer applies.

If then, capital punishment has no deterrent effect, as case study after case study has conclusively proven, then there remains only one reason for a return to executions in the name of the people. That is revenge. To those who exhort the Bible and invoke Leviticus 24:20 in that cause—"When one man injures his fellow countryman, it shall be done to him as he has done, fracture for fracture, eye for eye, tooth for tooth."—they might rather turn to the Sermon On The Mount:

> Ye have heard that it hath been said, An eye for
> an eye, and a tooth for a tooth; But I say unto
> you, That ye resist not evil; but whosoever shall
> smite thee on thy right cheek, turn to him the
> other cheek also.
> —St. Matthew 5, 38:39

On a final note, the extent to which society will go to cloak the anonymity and salve the conscience of the executioner who carries out the common will is ironic. Following is an excerpt from *Measures of Life*, by Richard M. Spolsky, in the March/April 1994 issue of *The Sciences* published by the New York Academy of Sciences:

> The days of the electric chair are almost over, the method of choice among modern executioners is the lethal-injection machine. The cosmetic benefits of this $30,000 contraption are obvious—no smoke, no sudden jolts, no unpleasant smell. But the real reason for the machine's growing popularity, one suspects, is not its effects on the prisoner but its effects on the executioner. The machine, as stipulated by law in some states, is outfitted with dual sets of syringes and dual stations, with switches for two people to throw at the same time. A computer with a binary-number generator randomizes which syringe is injected in the prisoner—and then erases the decision. No one will ever know who killed the prisoner—not even the computer.

Appendix

Aerial Photograph

This aerial photograph, taken in 1946, shows in detail the River Heights/Tuxedo area of Winnipeg. All of the numbers shown are placed with the left bottom corner of the square in which the numbers are inset indicating the precise spots mentioned in Mrs. Helen Berard's evidence at the trials and in her statements to police. No. 1 is the Berard home at 1064 Dudley Avenue where the birthday party took place. (Note the houses under construction behind the home, which pinpoints the date the aerial photograph was taken.) No. 2 is the intersection of Stafford Street and Corydon Avenue, where Mrs. Berard said Deacon flagged down a taxicab after they left the party. The taxicab then proceeded north as indicated by the white line to Academy Road and turned west, proceeding to Kenaston Boulevard. At this point Mrs. Berard gave several versions. As indicated in the double line on the right of the photograph, one version—and the most probable one—was that the taxi turned right onto Tuxedo Avenue and went toward Charleswood but then returned. No. 3 indicates the spot where Mrs. Berard told police she got out of the taxicab and where her footprints were found as well as one of Johann Johnson's wallets some time later. She then fled through the bush toward the south as indicated by the white line on the right. The line on the left leads to No. 4, the clearing where the stalled taxicab and the body of Johnson were found. No. 5 is the point on Kenaston Boulevard where Mrs. Berard's footprints were found a week later and where the handkerchief bearing the letter "J" was found. Mrs. Berard then continued down the railway track almost to Pembina Highway, which is off the photograph to the left. She was then given a lift back to Waverley Street as indicated by the top double line and appeared at the Winnipeg Dairy, indicated by No. 6, seeking directions. She then proceeded down Parker Avenue to the Zrudlo home at No. 7.

Winnipeg Free Press Illustration

This diagram, showing the spot where the body of Johann Johnson was found, appeared in the *Winnipeg Free Press* of April 1, 1946. Obviously constructed from a plan of a long forgotten subdivision, it gave the impression of a developed area, in contrast to the aerial photograph on pages viii-ix which shows faint trails in the bush. Only Kenaston Boulevard existed as a partly gravelled and little travelled muddy road. Throughout the trial police witnesses referred to certain intersections of streets on the diagram, leaving an impression in the minds of the jury that it was in fact an existing development.

Bibliography

Anderson, Frank W. *A Concise History of Capital Punishment in Canada.* Calgary: Frontier Publishing Ltd., 1973.

Canada, Department of Justice. *Capital Punishment: material relating to its purpose and value.* Foreword by Guy Fabreau. Ottawa: Queen's Printer, 1965.

Canada, Department of the Solicitor General. *Capital Punishment: New Material: 1965-1972.* Ottawa: Information Canada, 1972.

Canada. Library of Parliament Research Branch. *Capital Punishment in Manitoba.* Donald MacDonald, January, 1987, (unpublished).

Canada. Parliament. Joint Committee on Capital and Corporal Punishment and Lotteries, *Reports of the Joint Committee of the Senate and House of Commons on Capital Punishment,* June 27, 1956; *Corporal Punishment,* July 27, 1956; *Lotteries,* July 31, 1956. Ottawa: E. Cloutier, Queen's Printer, 1956.

Carrigan, D. Owen. *Crime and Punishment in Canada, A History.* Toronto: McClelland & Stewart Inc., 1991.

Cooper, David D. *The Lesson of the Scaffold.* London: Allen Lane, 1974.

Jayewarden, C.H.S. *The Penalty of Death: The Canadian Experience.* Lexington, Mass.: Lexington Books, 1977.

Hustak, Alan. *They Were Hanged.* Toronto: J. Lorimer, 1987.

Koestler, Arthur. *Reflections On Hanging.* New York: Macmillan, 1957.

Lawrence, John. *A History of Capital Punishment.* John Lawrence [pseudonym] with a comment on capital punishment by Clarence Darrow. New York: Citadel Press. 1960.

United Nations. Department of Economic and Social Affairs. *Capital Punishment:* Part I, report, 1960. Part II, developments, 1961 to 1965. New York: The Dept., 1968.

Other Sources

Manitoba Archives: Court of King's Bench Pockets 5/3855 (Lawrence Deacon); 5/3867 (Clarence Richardson); 5/3947 (Camille Allarie); 5/3951 (William Lusanko); 5/3970 (Walter Stoney); 5/3954 (Henry Malanik).

Manitoba Archives: Manitoba Court of Appeal records, St. James.

Manitoba Archives: *Winnipeg Free Press* and *Winnipeg Tribune* 1946-62.

National Archives Canada, Condensed summary of second trial of Lawrence Deacon, RG13 C-1, Vol. 1667, File Vol. 1 Part2.

National Archives Canada, Manitoba Court of Appeal written decision re Lawrence Deacon March 15, 1948, RG 13 C-1, Volume 1668, File Vol. 2 Part 2.

National Archives Canada, Report to the Secretary of State, The King v. Lawrence Deacon, RG 13 C-1, Volume 1668, Vol. 2 Part 1.

University of Manitoba, Elizabeth Dafoe Library, *Winnipeg Tribune* Archives.